Patricia M. Dechow
University of Michigan Business School

Catherine M. Schrand
Wharton School of the University of Pennsylvania

Earnings Quality

RESEARCH FOUNDATION

OF CFA INSTITUTE

ISBN 0-943205-68-9

Printed in the United States of America

July 2, 2004

Mission

The Research Foundation's mission is to encourage education for investment practitioners worldwide and to fund, publish, and distribute relevant research.

Biographies

Patricia M. Dechow is Carleton H. Griffin–Deloitte & Touche LLP Collegiate Professor of Accounting (Hons) at the University of Michigan Business School, where she teaches financial statement analysis. Previously, she was a faculty member at the Wharton School at the University of Pennsylvania. Professor Dechow's research focuses on the nature and purpose of accounting accruals, the use of accounting information in predicting stock returns, and the effects of analysts' forecasts on investors' perceptions of firm value. Her research has appeared in such journals as the *Journal of Financial Economics*, *Review of Accounting Studies*, and *Contemporary Accounting Research*. Professor Dechow is an editor of the *Accounting Review* and an associate editor of the *Journal of Accounting & Economics* and *Review of Accounting Studies*. She holds a bachelor of commerce degree from the University of Western Australia and a PhD in accounting and finance from the University of Rochester.

Catherine M. Schrand is associate professor of accounting at the Wharton School at the University of Pennsylvania, where she teaches financial accounting. Previously, she was an auditor and audit manager at KPMG Peat Marwick. Professor Schrand's research focuses on the risk management practices of nonfinancial companies and the relationship between a company's disclosure practices and its cost of capital. Her research has appeared in such journals as the *Journal of Finance*, *Accounting Review*, and *Journal of Financial Economics*. Professor Schrand serves on the editorial boards of the *Journal of Accounting & Economics* and the *Journal of Accounting Research,* and she serves as an *ad hoc* reviewer for numerous accounting and finance journals. She holds a BBA from the University of Michigan and an MBA and a PhD from the University of Chicago.

Contents

Foreword

Corporate fraud has dominated the financial news in recent years. The scandals at Enron Corporation, Tyco International, and WorldCom, to name but a few, underscore the will and ability of unscrupulous managers to defraud investors and other stakeholders. These scandals, together with less egregious conduct—some technically legal—call into question the reliability of reported earnings. It is thus timely that eminent scholars Patricia M. Dechow and Catherine M. Schrand explore the many issues surrounding earnings quality.

The authors begin with the premise that earnings should reflect a company's current and future operating performance and accurately annuitize its intrinsic value. As they point out, however, corporate managers occasionally manipulate earnings by altering real transactions, such as expenditures for research and development, or by shifting accruals.

Dechow and Schrand review the motivation of managers to manipulate earnings as well as their methods. As they note, managers engage in earnings manipulation typically to influence capital market transactions—such as equity offerings or mergers and buyouts—or to achieve favorable outcomes related to regulatory obligations, debt covenants, and executive compensation contracts.

In addition, the authors address a broad range of issues related to the quest for high-quality earnings data, including corporate governance and the Sarbanes–Oxley Act of 2002, voluntary disclosure, fair disclosure rules, and the response of investors to earnings management. In the process, they artfully explain the conceptual underpinnings of the central issues, and they present numerous facts and insights about earnings gleaned from scholarly research and statistical analyses, much of it their own. The result is a rigorous, comprehensive, and accessible analysis of earnings. Here are a few "sound bites" from their research:

- Earnings data perform better than cash flow data in predicting future earnings, and earnings backed by cash flows perform even better than earnings data alone.
- Earnings quality has deteriorated over time—as evidenced by the deteriorating relationship between stock prices and earnings.
- Earnings management is less prevalent among companies that employ Big Six auditors and have large independent blockholders.
- Abuse is more common among companies that have insider-controlled boards.

©2004, The Research Foundation of CFA Institute

- Analysts fail to recognize the time-series properties of earnings, which causes investors to misprice some stocks in predictable ways.
- Voluntary disclosures by management are systematically pessimistic, yet analysts fail to adjust for this bias.
- The United States, despite many high-profile scandals, has the least amount of earnings management.

These tidbits are but a small sample of an extraordinarily rich collection of facts and insights about earnings. Anyone who relies on financial statements or earnings reports would be well served to study this excellent monograph. The Research Foundation is especially pleased to present *Earnings Quality*.

Mark Kritzman, CFA
Research Director
The Research Foundation of
CFA Institute

Preface

Financial analysts are in the business of processing and interpreting information. Understanding the quality of earnings is an essential part of this procedure. A high-quality earnings number, as we define it, will do three things: It will reflect current operating performance; it will be a good indicator of future operating performance; and it will accurately annuitize the intrinsic value of the firm. Not all earnings are created equal. Earnings quality depends on the composition of the earnings, the stage of the company's life cycle, the time period, and the industry.

Determining earnings quality and its implications for firm value is complex. Understanding a company's quality of earnings requires expertise in finance, accounting, and corporate strategy and a strong knowledge of the industry in which the company operates and the governance mechanisms monitoring and rewarding employees and managers. An analyst armed with this knowledge provides the capital markets with an important value-added service.

This monograph begins with a discussion of how the current financial reporting system in the United States results in differences in earnings persistence and earnings quality. We show that the use of financial statement analysis can help predict these differences. We then turn to factors outside the financial reporting system that affect earnings quality. We describe the types of earnings management techniques companies use and when earnings management is most likely to occur. We discuss the role of directors, auditors, institutional investors, and analysts in monitoring management and improving earnings quality. Finally, we examine how investors respond to earnings and the importance of voluntary disclosures by managers as a means of supplementing the information in earnings. We summarize the information by documenting changes in earnings quality over time. And we provide explanations for the changes as well as discussion of standard setters' and regulators' influence on earnings quality. Throughout the monograph, we highlight trading strategies based on earnings quality; a list of sources that describe the strategies in detail is given in Appendix A.

We would like to thank Eli Amir, Amy Hutton, Gene Imhoff, Roby Lehavy, Sarah McVay, Greg Miller, Scott Richardson, Douglas Skinner, Richard Sloan, Jake Thomas, Irem Tuna, Peter Wysocki, and participants at the Information Quality and Markets Conference 2004, held in Australia at the University of New South Wales and the Sydney office of Ernst & Young. We are particularly grateful to the Research Foundation of CFA Institute for funding, to the Foundation's anonymous reviewer for helpful advice, and to Weili Ge for valuable research assistance.

1. Introduction

The United States has been home to some of the largest corporate frauds in the world. Enron Corporation's use of special-purpose entities enabled it to keep billions of dollars' worth of debt off its balance sheet, with investment bankers, lawyers, and accountants showing the company how. WorldCom used a simple scheme to capitalize more than $11 billion of expenditures as assets rather than expenses. Tyco International has been charged with failure to disclose millions of dollars of low-interest and interest-free loans to its executives. Qwest Communications International was forced to restate its revenues by $2.4 billion after the U.S. Securities and Exchange Commission discovered that its impressive revenue growth was mainly the result of swapping network capacity. Xerox Corporation boosted results by prematurely booking revenue from long-term leases of copiers and printers that it should have reported years later and by setting up "cookie jar" reserves during acquisitions that were later used to make up for shortfalls in operating results. Its restatement of earnings was more than $1.4 billion. Waste Management capitalized all sorts of expenditures that should have been expensed. And the list of financial accounting abuses goes on and on.

Why have accounting abuses become so prevalent in the United States in recent years? The volume of financial information provided by companies in the United States is among the highest in the world. The rules governing the production of the financial information are reputedly among the strictest in the world. Analysts in the United States are among the most accurate in the world at forecasting earnings, and the audit profession takes pride in the training and experience required of its professional staff. In addition, investor rights are among the strongest in the world. Certainly, the United States should be a safe place for an investor to purchase equity.

Perhaps part of the answer lies in the nature of accrual accounting and its interaction with economic cycles. Under accrual accounting, current experience is used to make accounting estimates for future periods and these estimates feed back into current-period earnings. Thus, the positive effect of real performance on earnings during booming economies is leveraged by the effects of optimistic forecasts concerning continued growth and investment opportunities. As the economy slows down, however, managers find it increasingly difficult to meet the high earnings hurdles set during the boom times. Downturns mean fewer sales, more bad debts, and more obsolete inventory.

The real decline in sales and earnings is exacerbated by the reversals of optimistic prior-period accruals. Some managers at this point use aggressive accounting—or, in the extreme, fraud—to avoid reporting a decline in earnings. The increased frequency of accounting abuses following the 1990s, which represent one of the longest periods of economic expansion in recent U.S. history, is not surprising.

The fundamental question is: Why do managers feel so much pressure to report continued growth in earnings? Managers may actually create part of the problem themselves by "guiding" analysts about future results and thus creating unrealistic expectations. When a manager's reputation is on the line, earnings management (viewed as "temporary") may seem like a low-cost way to avoid admitting a mistake. Corporate culture and management compensation packages also influence accounting choices. Divisional managers often feel intense pressure to meet targets set by top management. Stock option compensation can create incentives for top managers to set unrealistic targets for divisions to show "growth" so stock prices will continue to rise. Whether intentionally or unintentionally, managers have many incentives to "massage" earnings.

Our goal in this monograph is to provide structure for understanding "earnings quality." Earnings quality is contextual; it means different things to different financial statement users. The financial press refers to fraudulent reporting as an "earnings quality" problem. All financial statement users would probably agree with this definition. But the financial press also suggests that a company has an earnings-quality problem if earnings contain unusual items or lack transparency, even if reported earnings and the related disclosures are in accordance with generally accepted accounting principles. Standard setters, regulators, and auditors may disagree with the press on this point. Regulators generally view earnings to be of high quality when they conform to the spirit and the rules identified in GAAP. In contrast, creditors are likely to view earnings to be of high quality when they are easily convertible into cash flows. Compensation committees are likely to view earnings to be of high quality when they reflect managers' real performance and are little influenced by factors beyond management control. These examples illustrate that the decision maker's objective and the role of earnings in the decision model drive the definition of earnings quality.

We focus on the use of earnings as a measure of company performance. Specifically, we take the position that a high-quality earnings number will do three things: It will reflect current operating performance; it will be a good indicator of future operating performance; and it will accurately annuitize the intrinsic value of the company. Chapter 2 describes the concept of earnings quality in more detail.

An important point is that some companies, by the nature of their business, will have low-quality earnings even in the absence of intentional earnings manipulation. For high-growth companies, companies with intangible assets or complex transactions, and companies in volatile business environments, even accounting numbers that faithfully follow the spirit of GAAP may not provide an earnings number that is a good indicator of future cash flows. In these cases, the current financial reporting model, rather than intentional earnings management or poor monitoring, is to blame for low-quality earnings. Thus, we begin by looking at earnings-quality issues associated with the inherent strengths and weaknesses of the accrual accounting system for measuring performance. We leave an examination of the opportunities for purposeful manipulation of the numbers for later chapters.

In Chapters 3 and 4, we focus on how practitioners can use the financial statements to improve their assessment of earnings quality. Chapter 3 shows that decomposing earnings into the cash and accrual components can help an analyst predict future earnings and intrinsic value. Chapter 4 shows that the calculation of specific financial statement ratios and the isolation of specific earnings components can help an analyst understand current performance, predict future performance, and assess firm value.

We turn our attention to earnings manipulation and its effect on earnings quality in Chapter 5. When managers manipulate earnings, they are intentionally trying to hide current performance; the result is that current earnings are not indicative of future performance or intrinsic value. The critical issue is whether earnings management can be detected before the accrual accounting system catches up with the company and managers are forced to reverse the manipulated accounts. We provide research results on the accounts most likely to be manipulated as well as the circumstances or catalysts that are most likely to provide incentives for earnings management. We also provide some international comparisons and give some perspective on the extent of earnings management in the United States compared with that in other countries.

In Chapter 6, we discuss research evidence on the role of monitoring and its effectiveness in improving earnings quality. The Sarbanes–Oxley Act of 2002 is predicated on the assumption that stronger corporate governance will change corporate cultures and reduce accounting abuses. New rules on auditor independence aim to stop auditors from compromising audit quality for consulting fees. Strict separation of corporate finance and research in investment banking and fair disclosure rules aim to increase the independent scrutiny provided by analysts. These changes all indirectly affect earnings quality.

Chapters 7 and 8 address investor reactions to earnings news and the role of management guidance in improving investor and analyst understanding of the quality of earnings. Additional disclosure by management is more valuable when earnings are of low quality (i.e., when earnings do not reflect operating performance). We evaluate whether management guidance improves the reliability and predictability of earnings. We also examine whether managers are strategically self-serving in their disclosure choices, and we highlight where such strategic behavior is most likely to occur.

Finally, Chapter 9 shows that, not surprisingly, earnings quality has been declining over the past 40 years. Various explanations for the decline are investigated, but the evidence consistently shows that the decline is related to the increasing number of companies reporting losses and to "nonrecurring" special items. The growing frequency of nonrecurring charges has also led to an increase in the reporting of *pro forma* earnings. We discuss the types of charges excluded from *pro forma* earnings and managers' incentives to report this non-GAAP number.

Throughout this monograph, we assume that the stock market is competitive but not always efficient with respect to public information. We assume that information-processing costs can prevent prices from perfectly reflecting all public information. In addition, investors do not always behave rationally, so prices may deviate from fundamental values. Both of these factors imply that gains are possible from analyzing financial statements and understanding the quality of earnings. Many of the authors we cite developed trading rules that use differences in quality of earnings to identify under- or overpriced stocks. Appendix A summarizes the trading rules.

2. Defining Earnings Quality

Our focus is on earnings quality from the perspective of the analyst. The objectives of financial analysis are to evaluate the performance of the company, to assess the extent to which current performance is indicative of future performance, and based on this analysis, to determine whether the current stock price reflects intrinsic firm value. From this perspective, a high-quality earnings number is one that accurately reflects the company's current operating performance, is a good indicator of future operating performance, and is a useful summary measure for assessing firm value. We define earnings to be of high quality when the earnings number accurately annuitizes the intrinsic value of the firm. Such earnings are referred to as "permanent earnings" in the accounting literature (e.g., Black 1980; Beaver 1998; Ohlson and Zhang 1998). Another way to think about this concept is that earnings are of high quality when return on equity is a good measure of the internal rate of return on the company's current portfolio of projects.

An earnings number that represents the annuity of expected future cash flows is likely to be both persistent and predictable. Persistence and predictability in earnings alone, however, are not sufficient to indicate that earnings are high quality.[1] Managers often want earnings to be highly persistent and predictable because these characteristics can improve their reputations with analysts and investors. If such earnings do not annuitize the intrinsic value of the firm, however, the earnings are low quality. We illustrate this point with Enron Corporation in **Figure 2.1**. The lines show Enron's quarterly earnings per share (EPS) and earnings (per share) surprises from the first quarter of 1998 through the third quarter of 2001.

Figure 2.1 shows that Enron consistently had positive quarterly EPS and small positive EPS surprises to the end of 2000; thus, earnings were both predictable and persistent in the short run. [In Figure 2.1, note that the earnings surprise in September 2001 was based on *pro forma* earnings that excluded the $1.01 billion ($1.11 per share) nonrecurring charge.] As we now know, however, Enron managers were hiding losses in special-purpose entities throughout this period. Enron's earnings between 1998 and the second

---

[1] Chamberlain and Anctil (2003) discussed how some accounting rules, such as depreciation treatment, can increase persistence but reduce the usefulness of current earnings as a measure of permanent earnings. Rogerson (1997) and Reichelstein (2000) discussed theoretical depreciation rules that could lead to the reporting of permanent earnings from investments.

Figure 2.1.   Enron Quarterly Earnings per Share and Earnings Surprises, January 1998–September 2001

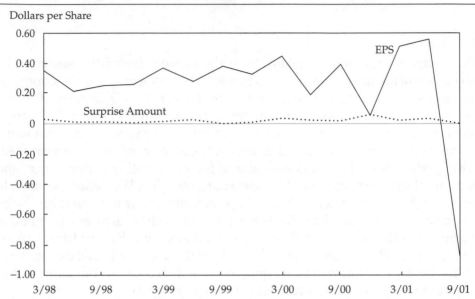

Note: Earnings surprise was calculated as actual earnings per share minus the consensus forecast of EPS.
Sources: Data from First Call/Thomson Financial and Compustat.

quarter of 2001 were not a good indicator of current performance, were not useful for predicting future performance (large losses occurred in the third quarter of 2001 and thereafter), and did not annuitize the intrinsic value of the firm. With hindsight, one can see clearly that Enron's earnings were of low quality under almost any understanding of the word "quality."

The point we want to make here is that earnings were also of low quality under our definition of quality. Greater earnings persistence is a meaningful definition for earnings quality only if earnings truly reflect performance during the period and if current-period performance persists in future periods. Persistence alone is not indicative, however, of high-quality earnings; the earnings stream must also reflect underlying intrinsic value.

Earnings quality can vary among companies as a function of accruals even in the absence of intentional earnings manipulation. Unlike the determination of cash flows, the determination of earnings requires estimations and judgments, and some companies require more forecasts and estimates than others. For example, companies in growing industries will typically have high accruals, which raises a question about reliability because accruals are likely

©2004, The Research Foundation of CFA Institute

to contain estimation errors. Estimation errors reduce earnings persistence (because they must be corrected in future earnings) and are irrelevant for valuation. Therefore, large accruals (of either sign) can indicate great underlying volatility in the company's operations and low-quality earnings (under our definition), even when the company is complying with generally accepted accounting principles (GAAP) and is not acting opportunistically.

Companies with extensive growth options are also likely to have low-quality earnings under our definition. For example, an analyst following a biotechnology company may find that current earnings are of little use in terms of predicting future earnings or intrinsic value. The value of such a company may depend totally on the success of a particular drug. We consider such a company to have low-quality earnings because today's earnings are practically irrelevant for evaluating current performance, predicting future performance, or determining firm valuation. In this case, low-quality earnings are simply the fault of the financial reporting system and how it captures (or does not capture) certain transactions or events.

Many would argue that volatility is a natural part of running a business and should be reflected in earnings. Although we agree, it is important to consider different types of volatility. If implemented properly, accrual accounting should result in an earnings number that reflects the underlying economic variation in the company's operations. It should smooth cash flow volatility, however, that does not reflect variation in underlying company performance. For example, when a company purchases inventory for $90, cash flow declines by $90 but earnings are not affected because the inventory is capitalized as an asset. In the next period, cash flow will increase by the value of the inventory sold—say, $120. Earnings, however, will increase by, in this case, $30. Which numbers better reflect the company's performance over the two periods: cash flows of –$90 and +$120 or earnings of $0 and $30? We believe that cash flows are excessively volatile and do not reflect current or future performance as well as earnings do. Thus, accruals can mitigate volatility and negative serial correlation in cash flows that are irrelevant for valuation.

But the benefit of accruals for smoothing irrelevant volatility comes at a cost. Accrual accounting opens the door to opportunistic short-run income smoothing that can lead to future restatements and write-downs (e.g., Enron). Earnings quality can be improved when accruals smooth out value-irrelevant changes in cash flows, but earnings quality is reduced when accruals are used to hide value-relevant changes in cash flows. Distinguishing between these two types of accrual adjustments is critical to financial analysis. As we discuss in Chapter 3, an astute analyst cannot focus on earnings alone. To assess earnings quality, the analyst must evaluate the company's cash flow statement and balance sheet in conjunction with the income statement.

The issue of whether the "smoothing effect" of accruals moves earnings closer to or farther from permanent earnings is a critical tension in accounting standard setting. To use the terminology of standard setters, this tension is the trade-off between relevance and reliability. A *reliable* number is one that is verifiable and reasonably free of error or bias. A reliable number involves little estimation or judgment. A *relevant* number is one that is timely and has predictive value for valuation. A number that is, in theory, relevant for valuation will not be useful if it is not reliable. Assume, for example, that company managers could provide an estimate of permanent earnings. Given the information that managers have, this number would be extremely relevant. But because such a number would be unverifiable, it would be unreliable, so it would be of little use in valuation. Similarly, a reliable number is not necessarily relevant.

Both relevance and reliability are needed to have high-quality earnings, but the relative importance of these two factors is difficult to articulate. What can be stated is that one company's earnings are of higher quality than those of another company if the earnings of the first company are both more reliable and more relevant.

Earnings Quality and Valuation

In theory, equity value equals the sum of expected future net dividends discounted at the company's cost of capital:[2]

$$P_e = \sum_{t=1}^{\infty} \frac{D_t}{(1 + r_e)^t},$$ (2.1)

where

P_e = price of company's equity

D_t = dividends to common equityholders less any net equity issuance

r_e = company's cost of equity capital

If dividends or free cash flows are the relevant attributes for valuation, then an obvious question is why analysts should care about the quality of earnings for valuation. Why shouldn't analysts simply focus on forecasting cash flows to compute a target price and use the forecast to make stock recommendations?

Analysts should care about earnings quality for equity valuation—despite the fact that finance textbooks generally focus on discounted cash flow models—for two reasons. First, from a practical perspective, earnings are frequently used in valuation. A survey by Block (1999) showed that 46 percent of

---

[2]The model in Equation 2.1 can be restated in terms of free cash flow (cash flows to all those financing the company).

analysts never use present value techniques in determining valuation and that only 11.8 percent of analysts view the dividend-discount model (DDM) as important. When the surveyed analysts were asked to rank their key valuation inputs, they ranked earnings first and dividends last. Many of the surveyed analysts said they use price/earnings multiples to value companies, and earnings quality was ranked as an important determinant of the P/E multiple.

Second, from a theoretical perspective, Ohlson (1995) showed that the DDM can be written in terms of earnings and book value (see also Preinreich 1938; Edwards and Bell 1961; Kay 1976). In this form, the model is referred to as the "residual income model." We will provide a brief reconciliation of the DDM with the residual income model.

The first step in converting the DDM to the residual income model is to assume "clean" surplus. Clean surplus accounting implies that the book value of equity increases only with net income, decreases with dividend payments, and increases or decreases with stock-related transactions:

$$CE_t = CE_{t-1} + NI_t - D_t, \qquad (2.2a)$$

or

$$D_t = NI_t - (CE_t - CE_{t-1}), \qquad (2.2b)$$

where CE_t is the company's common shareholders' equity (i.e., its book value) at date t and NI_t is the company's net income for the period ending at t (comprehensive net income). For each forecast of dividends in the DDM, earnings and book values can be substituted. And some simple algebra supplies the DDM rewritten as the residual income model:

$$P_e = CE_0 + \sum_{t=1}^{\infty} \frac{(NI_t - r_e CE_{t-1})}{(1 + r_e)^t}, \qquad (2.3)$$

where P_e is the estimated market value (price) of common equity at Date 0 and CE_0 is the company's common shareholders' equity at Date 0. The second term is the present value of residual income that the company generates over a finite forecast horizon. Residual income is equal to the company's earnings (NI_t) in excess of a rate that is required for the company to earn its cost of capital ($r_e CE_{t-1}$). Equation 2.3 indicates that a company's equity should be valued at its book value unless the company generates residual income. If residual income is positive, then firm value is greater than book value.[3]

---

[3]Dechow, Hutton, and Sloan (1999) showed that the average persistence of residual income across a broad cross-section of companies is 0.62. This figure suggests that residual income is slowly mean reverting.

The ratio of market value to book value (MV/BV) and P/E can also be expressed in terms of residual income (Fairfield 1994). If both sides of the residual income model are scaled by book value of equity, the result is the MV/BV:

$$\frac{P_e}{CE_0} = 1 + \sum_{t=1}^{\infty} \frac{(\text{ROE} - r_e)(CE_{t-1}/CE_0)}{(1+r_e)^t},$$ (2.4)

where ROE is return on equity. And the P/E multiple is

$$\frac{P_e}{NI_0} = \frac{1+r_e}{r_e}\left[1 + \sum_{t=1}^{\infty} \frac{\Delta RI_t}{(1+r_e)^t NI_0}\right] - \frac{D_0}{NI_0},$$ (2.5)

where ΔRI_t is the change in residual income between dates $t-1$ and t.

These expressions illustrate that valuations based on these ratios require strong assumptions about growth rates and profitability within the comparison group. Comparing companies on the basis of MV/BV assumes that (1) the quality of the accounting rules that produce book value, (2) the abnormal return on equity $(ROE - r_e)$, (3) discount rates, and (4) forecasted growth in book value (CE_{t-1}/CE_0) are constant across companies. Comparing companies on the basis of P/Es assumes that (1) the quality of accounting rules that produce earnings, (2) the dividend payout ratio (D/NI), (3) discount rates, and (4) the growth in residual income are constant across companies (see also Lundholm and Sloan 2003).

In summary, the use of earnings in various valuation models can be theoretically justified. The higher the quality of current earnings, the more useful the earnings data as a forecasting metric and the more accurate the valuation. The critical question is whether analysts are better off forecasting earnings and using these forecasts in an earnings-based model or ignoring earnings and focusing on forecasting cash flows as an input in a cash flow–based model. We explore research examining this empirical issue in the next section.

Earnings vs. Cash Flows

People usually have strong beliefs when it comes to whether earnings or cash flows are more useful for valuation. The difference between earnings and cash flow data is the accrual adjustments. Therefore, the ultimate question is whether accrual data contain information that improves valuation forecasts.

Most practitioners and academics agree that cash flows are more reliable than earnings. Unlike earnings that contain accruals, cash flows are not estimated. In addition, for a company to manipulate cash flows, it must incur real costs (although the manipulation of its cash balance by the Italian dairy-foods giant Parmalat appears to be an exception to this rule). Companies can "manage" the classification of cash flows as operating, financing, and investing activities in the cash flow statement. For example, WorldCom moved negative cash flows from the operating section to the investment section by capitalizing costs as long-term assets. Companies can also manage real activities to affect cash flows. For example, Sunbeam Corporation "encouraged" wholesalers to take delivery of barbecue grills in December that normally would have been purchased in the following year (a practice known as "channel stuffing"). But considering the estimations involved in determining earnings and the opportunities that exist for companies to manage earnings, cash flows can be thought of as relatively reliable.

The issue that divides people is whether the relevance of earnings for valuation compared with the relevance of cash flows dominates any weaknesses created by the relative lack of reliability in earnings. Addressing this question leads inevitably to a discussion of the purpose of accruals (and thus earnings). Storey and Storey (1998) noted a tension in accounting thought and practice between two widely held and essentially incompatible views about income:

1. Income is an enhancement of wealth or command over economic resources.
2. Income is an indicator of the performance of an enterprise and its management.

The first view is consistent with a "balance sheet" perspective on the financial statements as a whole. From this perspective, the objective of accounting is to measure assets and liabilities at some representation of market or fair value and the income statement represents changes in these values. If accrual adjustments reflect mainly transitory (unpredictable) revaluations of assets and liabilities, then bottom-line earnings are likely to be less useful than current cash flows for predicting future cash flows.

The second view is consistent with the revenue recognition principle and the matching principle. The revenue recognition principle requires that revenue be earned and realizable, and the matching principle requires delaying the recognition of costs until the revenue associated with the costs is recognized. If accrual adjustments reflect mainly the application of these two principles, then earnings will be a better measure of current performance than cash flows and a better measure of permanent earnings. In this case, earnings will be more useful than current cash flows in predicting future cash flows.

Current accounting standards, which dictate the measurement of earnings, reflect a mix of these two perspectives. Therefore, whether accruals improve the predictive ability of earnings relative to cash flows is not clear. Some accruals do and some do not. In practice, the incremental benefit of accruals is even less obvious. Accruals require estimation, and estimation error (either intentional or unintentional) reduces the ability of earnings to reflect future cash flows. Therefore, whether earnings or cash flows are more persistent and which one better reflects future cash flows are empirical questions.

Research into the relative merits of cash flows and earnings for valuation—that is, investigating which measure is of higher quality as we have defined it—uses various criteria for judging which is better. Earnings or cash flows are judged to be of higher quality when they are

1. more persistent and less volatile,
2. more strongly associated with future cash flow realizations, and
3. more strongly associated with contemporaneous stock price performance or market value.

Each of these criteria can be criticized. Using Criterion 1, for example, effectively assumes that persistent earnings improve the ability of earnings to capture value-relevant information. But consider a company that has reported $5 of earnings in each of the past few years. The earnings number is persistent and has low volatility, but it may not be relevant for measuring anticipated growth, which reduces its usefulness for valuation. Similarly, Criterion 2 assumes that predicting cash flows is useful for valuation, but actual future cash flows can be a noisy metric of value. Moreover, the researcher must specify a particular cash flow number to predict. The use of Criterion 3 as a benchmark for judging earnings quality assumes that markets are efficient and that stock prices quickly reflect all publicly available information. If investors fixate on one metric (either earnings or cash flows) and ignore information in another, then the stronger association indicates only that investors used a particular number in valuation, not that they should have.

To measure persistence, researchers generally estimate a regression of the future value of the variable on its current value. That is,

$$X_{t+1} = \alpha_t + \beta X_t + \epsilon_t. \tag{2.6}$$

The closer β is to 1, the more persistent the variable X_t is.[4]

---

[4]Literature on the time-series properties of annual earnings is extensive. Early studies include Ball and Watts (1972) and Watts and Leftwich (1977).

Table 2.1 illustrates the persistence of earnings and cash flow components (scaled by assets) for a sample of 56,940 company-years of reported cash flows and earnings between 1987 and 2002.[5] The persistence parameters represent the estimates of β in Equation 2.6. Table 2.1 indicates that, on average, earnings are more persistent than either cash flow from operations (CFO), free cash flow (FCF), cash flow from financing (CFF), or cash flow from investing (CFI). Therefore, if an analyst were forced to pick only one valuation model to use for all companies, then based on the persistence criterion, an earnings-based model would be the right choice. Table 2.1 also illustrates that the persistence of earnings declines for earnings subtotals that are reported farther down on the income statement because these amounts are more likely to include nonoperating items. Operating income has a persistence rate of 0.76, whereas bottom-line earnings have a persistence rate of 0.71.

Dechow (1994) evaluated earnings relative to cash from operations and net cash flows as a measure of company performance for the 1964–89 period. She found that earnings are less volatile than cash flows and that earnings are more persistent than cash flows (Criterion 1). She also documented that earnings have a higher association with contemporaneous stock returns than do cash flows (Criterion 3) and that earnings data are a better measure of company performance, particularly over short time horizons (i.e., quarterly and annual intervals).

Table 2.1. Persistence of Income Statement and Cash Flow Statement Items, 1987–2002

Item	Estimated Persistence Parameter
Sales	0.85
Operating income before depreciation	0.76
Operating income after depreciation	0.76
Pretax income	0.72
Earnings before special items	0.71
Earnings before extraordinary items	0.71
Cash flow from operations	0.65
Free cash flow	0.41
Cash flow from financing activities	0.30
Cash flow from investing activities	0.25

[5]Statement of Financial Accounting Standards (SFAS) No. 95 (FASB 1987) has required companies to report cash flows in a cash flow statement since 1987. Thus, the time period of this analysis uses a consistent measure of cash flows, which is more accurate than conversions inferred from changes in balance sheet accounts (Hribar and Collins 2002). FASB statements can be found at www.fasb.org/st/.

Several papers have directly examined the relative performance of cash flows and earnings for predicting future cash flows (Criterion 2). Finger (1994) examined the magnitude of forecast errors by using earnings and cash from operations to predict cash flows one year, four years, and eight years ahead. She found that when cash from operations is used, forecast errors are slightly lower than when earnings are used for predicting one-year-ahead cash flows. For the four-year-ahead and eight-year-ahead forecasts, however, earnings and cash flows are equally useful. Dechow, Kothari, and Watts (1998), using data for 1963–1992, showed that earnings are more useful than cash flows over long forecasting horizons and for companies with long operating cycles.

Barth, Cram, and Nelson (2001) found that *aggregate* earnings data are not more useful in predicting future cash flows than current cash flows but that decomposing the accrual component of earnings into the change in accounts receivable, change in accounts payable, change in inventory, and depreciation provides information that is useful for predicting future cash flows. They concluded that such accruals, which are consistent with the revenue recognition and matching principles, improve the predictive ability of earnings data relative to cash flows whereas more transitory and negative nonoperating accruals (such as special items) drive the result that aggregate earnings are less useful than aggregate cash flows. We will have more to say about special items in Chapters 7 and 9.

Penman and Sougiannis (1998) evaluated cash flows and earnings within the residual income valuation framework. They specified a valuation model that used earnings as the main input and two other models that used dividends or cash flows as the main input. They then examined which model produced a firm value closest to the observed actual market value of the firm (Criterion 3).[6] They concluded that "techniques based on forecasting GAAP accrual earnings yield lower valuation errors than those based on forecasting dividends or cash flows" (p. 347).[7]

In summary, research indicates that earnings are generally more persistent than cash flows. The results on the relative ability of earnings and cash flows to predict future cash flows are mixed. The key to understanding the predictive ability of earnings is an assessment of whether accruals represent

---

[6]They did not actually compute firm-specific values in their analysis. The model comparisons were based on portfolios of companies in order to average out both unexpected realizations and market inefficiencies across companies and over time.

[7]Lundholm and O'Keefe (2001) argued that the findings in Penman and Sougiannis were driven by different terminal value assumptions for the earnings and cash flow models, because both approaches should give the same result. Penman (2001b) provided a counterargument to this criticism. He argued that cash versus accrual accounting matters to valuation in the context of forecasting over a *finite* horizon.

an application of the revenue recognition and matching principles or an adjustment to the values of assets and liabilities reported on the balance sheet. If a large proportion of earnings represents nonoperating accruals that adjust the balance sheet (such as restructuring charges or gains and losses from sales of long-term assets), then aggregate earnings will probably not dominate current cash flows for predicting future cash flows and disaggregating earnings into its components will be important. Finally, for large samples of companies, earnings-based models outperform cash flow–based models for measuring firm value. This result is subject to a caveat, however: "Firm value" must be based on stock price. If it is not, the result may indicate that, although market participants are using earnings, on average, to value companies, it is not always the right thing to do.

3. Cash and Accrual Components of Earnings

The research evidence discussed in Chapter 2 suggests that earnings are, on average, more persistent than cash flows and that certain components of earnings are more persistent than others. But earnings are simply current-period revenues and expenses that are received and paid in cash plus accruals. A decomposition of earnings into the cash flow component and the accruals component, therefore, can provide insights into the persistence of each component and thus the quality of earnings overall.

The Accrual Anomaly

Sloan (1996) evaluated whether cash from operations and accruals have different implications for the persistence of future earnings (calculated as income from continuing operations divided by average assets). He was *not* testing the ability of earnings to forecast future cash flows. He was testing the ability of earnings or earnings components to forecast future earnings. He estimated the following regressions:

$$\text{Earnings}_{t+1} = \alpha + \beta \text{Earnings}_t + \epsilon_{t+1} \tag{3.1}$$

and

$$\text{Earnings}_{t+1} = \alpha + \gamma_1 \text{Accruals}_t + \gamma_2 \text{Cash from operations}_t + \epsilon_{t+1}. \tag{3.2}$$

Table 3.1, which provides his results, should be interpreted as follows. If a company earns $1.00 of earnings, then, on average, 84 cents will persist into next year's earnings. For each $1.00 of earnings that represents accruals, however, only 76.5 cents will persist into next year's earnings. For each $1.00 of earnings that represents operating cash flows, 85.5 cents will persist into next year's earnings. In other words, earnings that are backed by cash flows are more persistent than earnings that represent accruals.

An explanation of why the accrual component of earnings is less persistent than the cash flow component is that over- and understatements of accruals in the current period are adjusted via accruals in future periods. The recording and subsequent reversal of accrual misstatements result in higher volatility of accruals than of cash flows, which results in less persistent earnings (see, e.g.,

©2004, The Research Foundation of CFA Institute

Table 3.1. Regressions of Future Earnings Performance on Current Earnings Performance and the Cash Flow and Accrual Components of Earnings, Data for 1962–1991

Variable	Earnings$_t$ Only		Accruals and Cash Flows	
	Coefficient	*t*-Statistic	Coefficient	*t*-Statistic
Intercept	0.015	32.57	0.011	24.05
Earnings	0.841	303.98		
Accruals			0.765	186.53
Cash from operations			0.855	304.56

Notes: 40,679 company-years. All variables scaled by average assets.
Source: Tables 2 and 3 of Sloan (1996).

Dechow and Dichev 2002).[8] Misstatements of accruals may occur simply because managers have to make forecasts and judgments when determining accruals. Even if these estimates are unbiased, they will contain errors that require correction in future periods. Misstatements may also occur because managers have more flexibility to manipulate accruals than cash flows. Manipulating accruals requires only a journal entry; manipulating cash flows requires collusion with other parties or manipulation of transactions and/or their timing.

The Sloan study focused on whether investors understand that the quality of earnings is a function of whether the earnings are backed by cash flows or accruals. His evidence from returns to a trading strategy on a hypothetical portfolio suggests that investors fixate on earnings and do not consider the differential persistence of accruals and cash flows.[9] For this part of the study, he ranked companies on the basis of the magnitude of their accruals and hypothetically sold short companies that had high accruals and bought companies that had low accruals. The hedge return to this strategy was approximately 10 percent a year. Approximately 4.5 percentage points of this return occurred in the 3-day periods surrounding each of the four quarterly earnings announcements (i.e., it was earned over a total of 12 days). He interpreted these results as evidence that investors assumed these companies had the normal level of earnings persistence and did not realize the more transitory nature of accruals.

[8]Fairfield, Whisenant, and Yohn (2003a) proposed that the documented lower persistence of accruals is related to scaling accruals by *average assets*. An increase in net accruals mechanically implies a related increase in average assets, the scaler. An increase in operating cash flows, however, does not automatically imply an increase in ending assets because cash flows can be paid out as dividends or used to reduce liabilities. If the company is experiencing declining returns to growth, the scaling issue biases the Sloan model in favor of finding a lower persistence in earnings. Fairfield et al. showed that scaling by beginning assets (rather than average assets) supports this proposal. We discuss this point in more detail in a later section.
[9]The list in Appendix A provides the references for all the trading strategies reported in the monograph.

Several studies have provided evidence about whether relatively informed parties (including analysts, short sellers, institutional investors, creditors, and managers) understand the predictable effects of accruals documented by Sloan. Bradshaw, Richardson, and Sloan (2001) found that analysts, at best, only partially adjust their forecasts to correct for these effects. Richardson (2003) suggested that short sellers do not exploit the accrual anomaly. Collins, Gong, and Hribar (2003) investigated whether institutional investors trade on the accruals strategy. Their results suggest that institutional investors mute the effect of the accrual anomaly. Lev and Nissim (2002) provided evidence that institutions started to trade on the accrual anomaly strategy only after the publication of Sloan. Janes (2003) found that accruals are useful for predicting financial distress but that these predictable effects are not formally incorporated into debt covenants. Bhojraj and Swaminathan (2003) investigated whether relatively sophisticated bond market investors understand the information in a company's accruals. They found that bonds of companies with high accruals significantly underperform bonds of companies with low accruals. The performance differences ranged, depending on the accrual measure used to sort the companies, from 50 bps to 118 bps a year. Beneish and Vargus (2002) suggested that insiders profitably trade on the accrual anomaly. They documented that insiders of companies reporting low accruals tend to be net purchasers of the stock whereas insiders of companies reporting high accruals are net sellers.

Thus, the evidence to date suggests that relatively sophisticated users of financial statements do not fully understand that the accrual component of earnings is less persistent than the cash flow component but that the preparers of the financial statements do.

Reconciling the Evidence on Persistence

The results in Chapter 2 need to be reconciled with the results presented so far in this chapter. Earnings are, on average, more persistent than cash flows, but the cash flow component of earnings is more persistent than accruals. These two statements are not inconsistent because the persistence of earnings and cash flows varies with the magnitude of accruals (Dechow 1994).

This point can be seen graphically in **Figure 3.1** for 98,624 company-year observations from 1987 to 2001. The observations were ranked into deciles based on the magnitude of accruals (earnings less cash from operations). Decile 1 contains companies with large negative accruals, and Decile 10 contains companies with large positive accruals. The following regression models estimated the persistence of earnings and cash flows within each decile (with CFO = cash from operations):

Figure 3.1. Persistence of Earnings and Cash Flow from Operations as a Function of the Magnitude of Current Accruals, 1987–2001

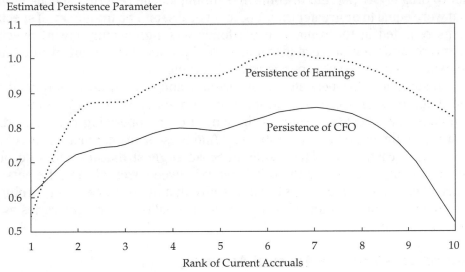

Notes: Cash flow from operations (CFO) scaled by assets. Rank of current accruals is the difference between earnings and CFO.

Source: Dechow and Ge (2003).

$$\text{Earnings}_{t+1} = \alpha + \beta\text{Earnings}_t + \epsilon_t \tag{3.3}$$

and

$$\text{CFO}_{t+1} = \alpha + \delta\text{CFO}_t + \epsilon_t, \tag{3.4}$$

where β is the earnings persistence parameter and δ is the cash flow persistence parameter.

When all observations were pooled, the average persistence of earnings was found to be 0.71 and that of cash flows, 0.65. As Figure 3.1 shows, earnings were more persistent than cash flows in 9 of the 10 deciles. The persistence of earnings and cash flows varied, however, with the level of accruals. The persistence of earnings was lower when accruals were large in absolute value. For example, in Deciles 1 and 10, earnings persistence was, respectively, approximately 0.6 and 0.8. In Decile 5, where accruals were small in absolute magnitude, earnings persistence was close to 1.0. Thus, earnings are more persistent than cash flows, on average, but large accruals of either sign reduce the persistence of earnings.

Decile 1 is the only decile in which cash flows were more persistent than earnings. This decile consisted of accruals that were large and negative. Approximately 47 percent of companies in this decile reported special items that were equal to or greater than 1 percent of assets. The frequency of special items reported in the remaining portfolios was significantly lower. Special items are, by definition, related to unusual or infrequent events and would thus be expected to reduce the persistence of earnings.

In summary, the persistence of earnings and of cash flows is related to the magnitude of accruals. The level of accruals depends on a number of company characteristics, such as the length of the operating cycle and the volatility of the underlying operations.[10] And these same company characteristics affect cash flows. The results in Sloan suggest that investors do not appear to fully understand the relationship between accruals and the persistence of earnings, but analysts should realize that the persistence of earnings varies with the magnitude of accruals, so the quality of earnings varies as a function of accruals.

Understanding the Accrual Anomaly

Researchers have examined whether the accrual results documented by Sloan are driven by a specific set of accruals. Xie (2001) classified companies' accruals into a discretionary component and a nondiscretionary component by using a time-series model.[11] His results indicate that discretionary accruals are less persistent than nondiscretionary accruals (coefficient estimates of 0.57 versus 0.70). Moreover, a hypothetical trading strategy of buying companies in the lowest decile of discretionary accruals at the end of year t and selling short companies in the highest decile of discretionary accruals earned a return of 11 percent over the following year $(t + 1)$. Following the same strategy but basing the portfolios on nondiscretionary accruals earned a return of only 2.3 percent. Thus, isolating discretionary accruals led to higher abnormal returns.[12] Xie did not compare either of his trading strategies with one based on total accruals. Therefore, we cannot know whether this decomposition is better than using total accruals, but the difference in the returns for the two trading strategies suggests that it is.

---

[10]See, for example, Dechow; Dechow and Dichev; Minton, Schrand, and Walther (2002).

[11]Xie used the Jones (1991) model to classify companies. This model, which is commonly used in the accounting literature, measures the nondiscretionary portion of accruals on the basis of other company financial characteristics, such as changes in revenues and fixed-asset balances. We describe the Jones model in more detail in Chapter 5.

[12]Xie was building on work by Subramanyam (1996a) showing that discretionary accruals not only are priced by the market but also appear to be overpriced.

In a related vein, Dechow and Dichev also decomposed accruals into two types. They argued that "good" accruals are those that match past, present, or future cash flows and "bad" accruals are the result of estimation error or corrections of previous estimation errors. Using a statistical model to identify the two types of accruals, they found that companies with large accruals tend to have large estimation errors. This finding helps explain Sloan's finding that the persistence of earnings is lower when earnings consist mainly of accruals. When accruals are large in magnitude, they are likely to contain significant estimation error, which reduces the persistence of earnings.

Thomas and Zhang (2002) and Hribar (2001) decomposed Sloan's accrual measure into various asset and liability components. Thomas and Zhang documented the following hedge returns from trading on the basis of a specific accrual:

- change in current assets, 9.09 percent,
- change in current liabilities, 1.34 percent,
- depreciation, 4.74 percent,
- change in accounts receivable, 3.67 percent,
- change in accounts payable, –2.74 percent,
- change in inventory, 11.39 percent, and
- change in other accruals, 3.78 percent.

These results suggest that changes in inventory are the key drivers of the accrual anomaly.

Thomas and Zhang attempted to disentangle two explanations of why inventory changes are a strong driver of the accrual anomaly. One explanation is that high inventory levels reflect an intentional delay in the expensing of inventory costs, which is an issue of earnings quality. If this is the case, Thomas and Zhang expected increases in the finished goods component of inventory (which is indicative of inventory not being sold or being written down) to have the biggest impact on the anomaly. The second explanation is that managers in the study overinvested in inventory and neither the management nor the market realized the declining return to this investment. If this is the case, Thomas and Zhang expected increases in the raw materials component of inventory to have the biggest impact on the anomaly. The evidence they found is mixed but is more consistent with the overinvestment explanation. Based on this work, investors are ignoring a fundamental signal: Unusual increases in inventory are bad news (see also Abarbanell and Bushee 1998).

Rather than decomposing accruals into types based on statistical models or balance sheet designations to examine differences in persistence among accrual types, Hanlon (2003) investigated the role of differences between book income and taxable income as an indicator of the persistence of accruals, cash flows, and earnings. Positive book–tax differences mean that book income (accrual income) is higher than taxable income, which is more cash based. Negative book–tax differences mean that book income is lower than taxable income. Hanlon noted that this situation usually indicates that the company has expenses that cannot be taken as tax deductions (e.g., reserves and accruals based on estimates) and that some of these expenses are likely to be transitory in nature (e.g., special one-time items). She documented that large absolute book–tax differences indicate less persistent earnings, cash flows, and accruals. Tests of market pricing suggest that investors correctly interpret large positive book–tax differences as an earnings-quality "red flag" but that investors fail to use the information in negative book–tax differences. Returns to the accrual anomaly can be increased by taking this information into account.

Desai, Rajgopal, and Venkatachalam (2004) had a different perspective on the accrual anomaly. They claimed that high-accrual companies are likely to be "glamour" stocks with low ratios of cash flow to price (CF/P) and low-accrual companies are likely to be "value" stocks with high CF/Ps.[13] Thus, the market has strong expectations for future growth for companies with high accruals and weak expectations for companies with low accruals. Consistent with this explanation, Desai et al. showed that, after CF/P was controlled for, future returns were not related to accruals.[14]

Barth and Hutton (2004) investigated the relationship between the accrual anomaly and analysts' earnings forecast revisions. In their sample, trading strategies based on accruals (buying companies with abnormally low accruals and shorting companies with abnormally high accruals) and on forecast revisions (buying companies with positive forecast revisions and shorting companies with negative forecast revisions) generated returns of, respectively, 15.5 percent and 5.5 percent when implemented independently. A combined strategy that used forecast revisions to refine the strategy based on the accrual anomaly generated a return of 28.5 percent. Thus, companies with consistent signals about earnings quality—high accruals and negative forecast revisions or low accruals and positive forecast revisions—have less persistent earnings.

Minton, Schrand, and Walther (2002) investigated whether the returns to Sloan's accrual strategy can be improved by considering cash flow volatility. Companies with more volatile cash flows are expected to make larger accrual adjustments, so observing high accruals in these companies is not unusual

---

[13]See Lakonishok, Schleifer, and Vishny (1994) for the introduction of these terms.

[14]Desai et al. made the important point that their measure of CF/P is not the same as that traditionally used in the finance literature. Lakonishok et al. and subsequent studies adjusted earnings only for depreciation to measure cash flows. But Desai et al. also adjusted for changes in working capital accruals.

and is less likely to be an indication of poor earnings quality than observing high accruals combined with low cash flow volatility. Companies with low cash flow volatility, however, should have fewer timing and matching problems, and their accrual adjustments should be smaller. Observing high accruals in companies with low cash flow volatility is, therefore, an earnings-quality red flag. The results of Minton et al. indicate that the returns to the accrual anomaly are higher for companies with low historical cash flow volatility.

Extending the Definition of Accruals

Fairfield, Whisenant, and Yohn (2003b) suggested that the accrual anomaly arises from the effect of asset growth on persistence. They documented (see their Table 3 and note 12) that if no growth occurs in net operating assets [i.e., accounts receivable; inventory; other current assets; property, plant, and equipment (PP&E); intangible assets; and other long-term assets minus accounts payable, other current liabilities, and other long-term liabilities], then about 78 percent of return on assets (ROA) is expected to persist into the next year. If growth does occur in net operating assets, however, the persistence of ROA declines to 73 percent. Controlling for growth in net operating assets, they found that persistence of the cash flow and accrual components of ROA is the same. Long-term accruals (i.e., changes in PP&E, intangible assets, and other long-term assets minus the change in other long-term liabilities) and short-term operating accruals both affected the persistence of ROA.

Because Fairfield et al. (2003b) did not find a difference between the persistence of the cash flow and accrual components of ROA after they controlled for growth, they suggested:

> the lower persistence of accruals relative to cash flows from operations (documented in Sloan) is more likely to result from the conservative bias in accounting principles or the lower rate of economic profits that result from diminishing marginal returns to new investment opportunities, or both. (p. 355)

Because they found that growth in long-term accruals as well as in short-term operating accruals drives the lower persistence of ROA, they also stated:

> the lower persistence of accruals [documented in Sloan] is less likely to result from other features of accruals, such as their susceptibility to manipulation by management. (p. 355)

This last statement reflects an assumption that long-term accruals are less subject to manipulation than short-term accruals.

Richardson, Sloan, Soliman, and Tuna (2003, 2004), challenging the interpretation provided by Fairfield et al., argued that long-term assets are also accruals and are also subject to estimation error and managerial manipulation.

Richardson et al. decomposed accruals into working capital accruals, noncurrent net operating accruals, and net financial assets, and they showed that the anomaly is driven by the accruals most subject to estimation error. They also found evidence that companies with large changes in their net operating assets are more likely to be subject to U.S. Securities and Exchange Commission enforcement actions, which is consistent with the theory that aggressive accounting (rather than conservative accounting) explains the lower earnings persistence.

Taking a different perspective, Richardson and Sloan (2003) suggested that companies with large increases in working capital assets or noncurrent net operating assets are probably raising financing. So, they investigated whether cash from financing (as reported in the statement of cash flows) predicts future returns. They found that when companies raise financing (through either debt or equity) and invest it in net operating assets, future stock returns are low. If the financing is used to pay down debt or repurchase equity, however, the new financing has no relationship to future returns.

Richardson and Sloan's results suggest a number of interpretations. One implication is that companies overinvest in assets; therefore, the marginal return on new financing used to purchase assets leads to a lower average return on new investment and a decline in ROA. This decline in ROA is not anticipated by investors and leads to future declines in stock returns (which is consistent with the view of Fairfield et al.).

A second interpretation (e.g., Rangan 1998; Teoh, Welch, and Wong 1998a, 1998b) is that when companies raise financing, they temporarily boost accruals to improve their performance. Returns will be lower when the accruals eventually reverse.

A third interpretation (e.g., Dechow, Hutton, and Sloan 2000; Bradshaw, Richardson, and Sloan 2003) is that analysts working for investment banks are more likely to "hype" the stock of growing companies. Investors believe the hype, so they are subsequently disappointed when earnings do not meet their overly optimistic expectations.

Summary

Earnings are more persistent than cash flows, on average, but the cash flow component of earnings is more persistent than the accrual component. The persistence of both earnings and cash flows is related to the magnitude of accruals. The magnitude of accruals depends on a number of company characteristics, such as the company's stage in its life cycle, the length of its operating cycle, and the volatility of its underlying operations. And these same company characteristics affect cash flows.

Results of research on the accrual anomaly suggest the following:

- Investors do not understand that accruals are less reliable than cash flows. Accruals are measured with error, and this measurement error is irrelevant for valuation. The error in accruals could be the result of intentional earnings management, bad accounting standards, or unintentional estimation error. Whatever the cause, it reduces the persistence of earnings.
- Investors misunderstand the implications of past growth for future performance. Large positive accruals reflect investment in operating assets, and this investment is usually a consequence of raising financing. Overly optimistic estimates on the part of analysts and investors about the company's future growth opportunities lead to an inflated current price and future underperformance.

4. Financial Statement Components

Recall from Chapter 2 that our definition of a high-quality earnings number is one that is persistent and reflects permanent earnings. That is, high-quality earnings are a good indicator of the expected future cash flows to be generated by the company and, therefore, are relevant for equity valuation. Chapter 3 indicated the importance of decomposing earnings into cash flow and accrual components. In this chapter, we focus on other decompositions of the financial statements that can help an analyst assess earnings quality. Much of the research in financial statement analysis focuses on the persistence of return on equity (earnings scaled by the book value of equity) rather than a raw earnings number because ROE is of key interest to equity investors. The higher the quality of ROE, the better ROE reflects the internal rate of return on the company's projects.

Decomposing ROE

Fairfield, Sweeney, and Yohn (1996) investigated whether the persistence of ROE can be predicted more accurately by disaggregating the income statement and focusing on individual line items than by using only net earnings. First, they estimated the following regression to ascertain how current ROE (in the aggregate) explains future ROE:

$$\text{ROE}_t = \alpha + \beta \text{ROE}_{t-1} + \epsilon_t. \tag{4.1}$$

They then decomposed ROE into components and investigated which components explain future ROE. **Table 4.1** presents the coefficient estimates (and standard deviations) for 10 series of seven-year rolling regressions for 1973–1988.

The first regression indicated that approximately 66.4 percent of ROE persists to the next year. The second regression (the full model) indicated that decomposing ROE into its components better explains future ROE. The adjusted R^2 of the model—a measure of its explanatory power—increased from 42 percent to 49 percent. Moreover, the coefficient estimates on the earnings components are not all equal to 0.66. Thus, the persistence of the various components is different from the average persistence of ROE. The coefficient estimates on the operating components are similar (not statistically different from one another), which suggests that, on average, these sources

Table 4.1.   Average Coefficient Estimates and Standard Deviations for Regressions of ROE on Components of Prior ROE, Data for 1973–1988

Variable	ROE$_{t-1}$ Only		Full Model	
	Coefficient	Standard Deviation	Coefficient	Standard Deviation
Intercept	0.042	0.004	0.029	0.005
ROE	0.664	0.023		
Operating income components				
Gross margin			0.636	0.022
SG&A			0.639	0.022
Depreciation			0.629	0.073
Interest			0.621	0.019
Minority interest			0.615	0.078
Nonoperating income			0.548	0.037
Special items			0.123	0.019
Income taxes			0.445	0.028
Discontinued operations			0.003	0.028
Extraordinary items			0.153	0.058
Adjusted R^2	42.3%	0.029	49%	0.023

Note: SG&A = selling, general, and administrative expenses.
Source: Table 2 of Fairfield, Sweeney, and Yohn (1996).

of ROE can be treated as a group when forecasting future ROE. The coefficient estimates on the nonoperating sources of ROE, however, are significantly lower than those on the operating components, which implies that they are less persistent. Therefore, separating nonoperating income, income taxes, earnings associated with discontinued operations, and extraordinary items is important when forecasting future ROE.

Additional research has focused on decomposing ROE into its operating and financing components. The persistence and quality of ROE can be evaluated in terms of the persistence and quality of each of these components and the interaction between the two. Most research has focused on evaluating the persistence of the operating activity component of ROE rather than the financial leverage component. Financing is obtained from competitive markets, and researchers typically assume that companies pay a required rate of return (i.e., financing is a zero-net-present-value project). But operating activities create value because the company is more likely to have a competitive advantage in operating activities and, therefore, can earn economic rents.

The decomposition of ROE into the return generated by the company's *operating activities* and the return generated by its *financing activities* is illustrated in **Figure 4.1**.[15] We first discuss research into operating activities and then discuss the limited research on the impact of financing activities on ROE.

Figure 4.1.   Decomposition of ROE

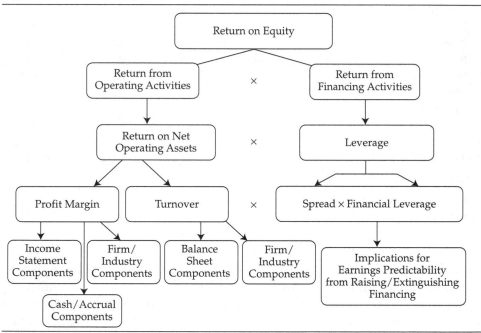

Notes:
NOA = Operating assets – Operating liabilities,
NOPAT = Net operating profit after taxes,
NFE = Net financial expense,
NFO = Financial liabilities – Financial assets,
Return on equity = Income/Equity,
Return on net operating assets (RNOA) = NOPAT/NOA,
Leverage = NFO/Equity,
Profit margin = NOPAT/Sales,
Turnover = Sales/NOA, and
Spread × Financial Leverage = (RNOA – After-tax NFE) × NFO/Equity.

[15]Nissim and Penman (2001), Penman (2001a), Lundholm and Sloan (2003), and Palepu, Bernard, and Healy (2000) provide detailed discussions of this decomposition.

Operating Activities. As Figure 4.1 shows, the return from operating activities (return on net operating assets) can be decomposed into a profit margin (the ratio of income to sales) and an asset turnover ratio (sales/net operating assets). The profit margin indicates the company's effectiveness in controlling costs of sales that are made. Turnover indicates the asset base required to generate a given level of sales and is thus considered to be a measure of operating efficiency.

Profit margin can be further disaggregated to measure specific costs on the income statement, such as cost of goods sold or selling, general, and administrative costs (SG&A), to highlight the source of a company's high (or low) profit margin. For example, one company might generate a high profit margin by charging a high markup for its products (achieving a high ratio of gross profits to sales) while another generates a high profit margin through low overhead costs.

Asset turnover also can be disaggregated. The disaggregation focuses on identifying which assets on the balance sheet are the source of the company's operating efficiency. For example, by separately measuring the receivables turnover and inventory turnover components of asset turnover, one can identify whether an improvement in operating efficiency results from better management of inventory or better collection of credit sales. For analysts, a better understanding of the sources of changes in income will lead to better predictions about the persistence of those changes into future ROE.

Nissim and Penman (2001) provided evidence of the persistence of return on net operating assets (RNOA). They ranked observations into deciles based on RNOA and reported the value of RNOA for each decile over the next five years. **Figure 4.2** shows that extreme RNOAs tend to revert to the mean.

Nissim and Penman (2001) decomposed RNOA into four components: core profit margin, other core items, unusual items, and asset turnover. This decomposition showed that asset turnover and core profit margin are highly persistent and unusual items and other core items are less persistent. These results suggest that the mean reversion in RNOA is driven by unusual items reported in income.

Nissim and Penman (2001) also found that changes in sales, profit margin, and asset turnover are strongly mean reverting. Using deciles of companies based on sales growth, they tracked subsequent sales growth for five years. **Figure 4.3** presents the results of their analysis. A company that has sales growth of 60 percent in one year is likely to have sales growth of only 20 percent in the following year and be almost back to the average sales growth of around 15 percent by the third year. The strong mean reversion indicates that to assume that extreme sales growth will continue at high historical growth rates for long periods of time is unrealistic.

Figure 4.2. Evolution of Net Operating Assets over Time: New York Stock Exchange and American Stock Exchange Companies Listed in Compustat, 1963–99

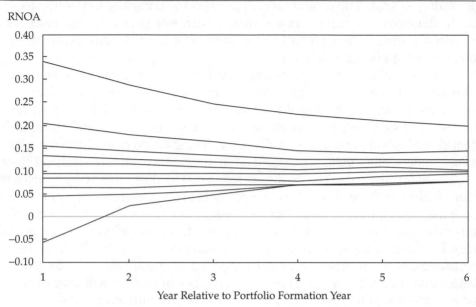

Year Relative to Portfolio Formation Year

Notes: Companies were ranked on the basis of RNOA in Year 0, placed into 10 portfolios, and then tracked for the following five years. The ranking was done in 1964, 1969, 1974, 1979, 1984, 1989, and 1994. The figure presents the mean of the portfolio medians.

Source: Figure 4 of Nissim and Penman (2001).

Fairfield and Yohn (2001) investigated whether decomposing the change in RNOA into change in profit margin and change in asset turnover is useful for predicting future changes in RNOA. They found that improvements in asset turnover lead to improvements in future RNOA but that changes in profit margin are uncorrelated with future changes in RNOA. In other words, improvements in operating efficiency are more persistent than improvements in profit margin. Improvements in profit margin are likely to be competed away.

Soliman (2003) suggested that asset turnover and profit margin must be evaluated against industry benchmarks. **Figure 4.4** provides a graphical representation of the trade-off between profit margin and asset turnover for various industries and illustrates that companies can achieve the same return on net operating assets in different ways. For example, grocery stores have a median RNOA of 20 percent; they achieve this return through high turnover (almost 8 times) despite low profit margins (less than 2 percent). The gold and

Figure 4.3. Evolution of Sales Growth over Time, 1963–99

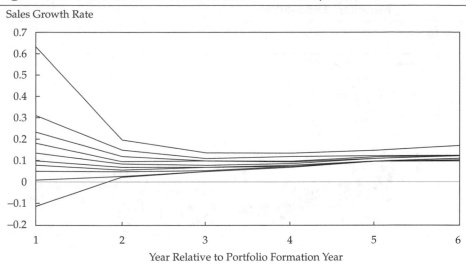

Notes: Companies were ranked on the basis of sales growth in Year 0, placed into 10 portfolios, and then tracked for the following five years. The ranking was done in 1964, 1969, 1974, 1979, 1984, 1989, and 1994. The figure presents the mean of the portfolio medians.

Source: Figure 4 of Nissim and Penman (2001).

silver ore industry also has a return on net operating assets of around 20 percent. Its profit margins are high (around 23 percent), however, and turnover is low (less than 1 time). Petroleum pipelines have high profit margins (38 percent) but low turnover (because of the capital costs in building a pipeline). The result is a median return on net operating assets of only 13 percent.

Given the differences among industries, Soliman suggested evaluating the sustainability of current ROE by examining deviations from industry averages. He showed that a company with a high RNOA, profit margin, or asset turnover relative to its industry median tends to have greater mean reversion in future RNOA, profit margin, or turnover than other companies. Furthermore, investors appear to realize that abnormal profit margins and RNOA are only temporary. Abnormal asset turnover, however, is not so well understood by investors. Soliman was able to generate positive abnormal returns from a trading strategy that used information in abnormal asset turnovers.

Financing Activities. Research into the role of financing activities on earnings (ROE) is limited, but a recent study by Nissim and Penman (2003) provided direct evidence about the implications of operating leverage and total

Figure 4.4. Industry-Level Combinations of Median Profit Margin and Asset Turnover, 1963–2000

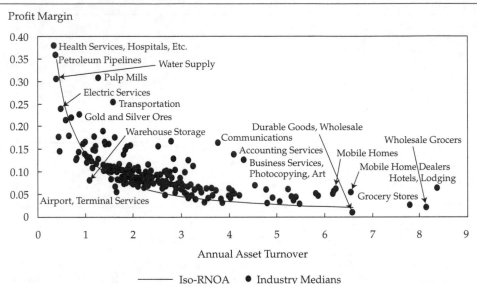

Notes: Points represent pairs of median profit margin and median asset turnover for 248 three-digit SIC industry groups. The curved line is the 14 percent iso-RNOA line—that is, the combination of profit margin and asset turnover that would result in an RNOA of 14 percent.

Source of Data: Soliman (2003).

financial leverage for future ROE. Operating leverage is defined as (Operating liabilities)/(Net operating assets). Operating assets are those required or generated as a part of operations (e.g., trade receivables; inventory; property, plant, and equipment) Operating liabilities include accounts payable, deferred revenues, restructuring liabilities, and pension liabilities. Total financial leverage is defined as [(Net financial debt + Operating liabilities)/Common equity]. Financial liabilities include bank loans, public debt, and short-term commercial paper minus deposits.

Nissim and Penman (2003) examined the effects of operating leverage, *OPLEV*, and total financial leverage, *TLEV*, on future profitability by using the following regressions:

$$\text{ROE}_{t+1} = \alpha + \gamma_1 \text{ROE}_t + \epsilon_{t+1} \tag{4.2}$$

and

$$\text{ROE}_{t+1} = \alpha + \gamma_1 \text{ROE}_t + \gamma_2 TLEV_t + \gamma_3 OPLEV_t + \epsilon_{t+1}. \tag{4.3}$$

Equation 4.2 measures the persistence of ROE from one period to the next and provides a benchmark. Equation 4.3 measures the association between future profitability and total financial leverage and operating leverage after current profitability has been controlled for. **Table 4.2** provides the mean coefficient estimates for 38 yearly regressions with an average number of 1,562 observations a year for 1963–2000.

Table 4.2. Average Coefficient Estimates for Equations 4.2 and 4.3, Data for 1963–2000

Variable	ROE_t Only		Full Model	
	Coefficient	t-Statistic	Coefficient	t-Statistic
Intercept	0.028	6.195	0.028	6.679
ROE_t	0.623	34.48	0.614	35.06
OPLEV			0.014	5.55
TLEV			−0.005	−3.74
Adjusted R^2	30.3%		30.9%	

Source: Table 3 of Nissim and Penman (2003).

The coefficient of 0.623 on ROE in the first equation indicates that, on average, 62.3 percent of ROE persists to the next year. Recall that the Fairfield, Sweeney, and Yohn study found a persistence rate of approximately 66 percent for the 1973–88 period. In the full model shown in Table 4.2, the positive coefficient on *OPLEV* indicates that operating leverage is good news for a company and improves future profitability, after current profitability is controlled for. The negative coefficient on *TLEV* suggests an economically small association between total financial leverage and future profitability.

Nissim and Penman (2003) suggested that accounting distortions explain the positive relationship between *OPLEV* and future ROE. Higher operating leverage can occur because the company (1) accrues more expenses or defers revenue (i.e., the numerator increases) or (2) writes off assets (i.e., the denominator decreases). Either scenario is likely to cause a temporary decline in current earnings, so future earnings are likely to rise. Further analysis shows that increases in estimated liabilities, such as restructuring or pension liabilities, lead to greater future improvements in ROE than do increases in contractual liabilities, such as accounts payable and taxes payable. Higher operating leverage is also associated with higher future price-to-book ratios after current profitability, growth, and risk are controlled for. This association is driven primarily by the effects of estimated liabilities on operating leverage.

The lesson of the Nissim–Penman (2003) study is that identifying the source of a company's leverage is important for understanding the quality of its earnings or ROE. Leverage obtained through outside financing generally does not improve a company's future ROE, whereas leverage associated with operating activities, because of accounting conservatism, is, on average, related to higher future ROE.

Other Financial Statement Decompositions

Abarbanell and Bushee (1997) investigated whether various ratios are useful for forecasting changes in earnings per share (EPS).[16] They focused on ratios that others have identified as potential "red flags" for poor earnings quality.[17] The variables were measured in such a way that the estimated coefficients were expected to be negative (i.e., the variables would increase the likelihood that future earnings would be lower). **Table 4.3** reports the way each variable was measured and its estimated relationship to changes in future EPS in a broad sample of companies in the 1980s.[18]

Table 4.3. Regression of Future Changes in EPS on Current Fundamental Signals, Data for 1983–1990

Signal	Measurement	Coefficient (predicted to be negative)	Note
Inventory	ΔInventory – ΔSales	–0.017*	
Accounts receivable	ΔAccounts receivable – ΔSales	0.009*	Wrong sign
Capital expenditures	ΔIndustry CAPEX – ΔCompany CAPEX	0.005*	Wrong sign
Gross margin	ΔSales – ΔGross Margin	–0.031*	
SG&A	ΔSG&A – ΔSales	–0.010	Insignificant
Effective tax rate (ETR)	(Average ETR for past 3 years – ETR_t) × ΔEPS_t	–0.594*	
Inventory method	0 for LIFO, 1 for FIFO or other	–0.006*	
Audit qualification	0 for unqualified, 1 for qualified	0.014	Insignificant
Labor force	–1 × (%Δ in sales per employee)	–0.026*	

*Significant at the 5 percent level.

Notes: CAPEX = capital expenditures; LIFO = last in, first out; FIFO = first in, first out.

Source: Table 2 of Abarbanell and Bushee (1997).

[16]References to the work of Abarbanell and Bushee in this section are to the 1997 paper unless otherwise stated.

[17]The red flags were identified from articles in such media as the *Wall Street Journal* and *Barron's* and from books and studies on earnings quality, such as O'Glove (1987) and Lev and Thiagarajan (1993).

[18]The analysis included a control for the current-period change in EPS, measured as $[(EPS_t - EPS_{t-1})/Price_{t-1}]$.

The inventory, gross margin, effective tax rate, inventory accounting method, and labor force signals—all had the predicted (negative) effect on one-year-ahead EPS. An increase in inventory greater than sales may indicate obsolete inventory and the potential for future write-offs. An increase in sales that does not result in a correspondingly large increase in gross margin may indicate increased competition or a change in the underlying relationship between fixed and variable costs. A significant change in the effective tax rate in the absence of a change in the federal tax rate is likely to be transitory and thus is a negative signal for future earnings. LIFO earnings are viewed as closer to economic earnings than FIFO earnings and thus a better measure of the true earning power of the company. Finally, generating more sales per employee is generally viewed as an increase in effective use of employees.

Abarbanell and Bushee had expected an increase in receivables greater than sales to indicate an insufficient allowance for doubtful accounts and the potential for future write-offs, but the results are inconsistent with this expectation. The estimated relationships between capital expenditures (CAPEX) and future EPS and between accounts receivable and future EPS are the opposite of the authors' predictions. The results imply that an increase in the ratio of accounts receivable to sales is, on average, indicative of a positive growth trend in sales, possibly because of an expansion of credit. As for CAPEX, they hypothesized that spending less than the industry average indicates that corporate management has cash flow concerns, which could lead to reduced future earnings. The results shown in Table 4.3 suggest, however, that EPS increases following decreases in industry-adjusted CAPEX. Abarbanell and Bushee suggested that the CAPEX result is driven by poorly performing companies. It could also be related to the overinvestment issues discussed in Chapter 3.

The SG&A and audit qualification signals are not significantly associated with changes in future EPS. Abarbanell and Bushee had expected that an increase in SG&A relative to sales could indicate a loss of managerial cost control or that an increase in SG&A could indicate an unusual sales effort that would positively affect future EPS. It appears that, on average, neither explanation dominates. The authors had expected an audit qualification to be negatively associated with changes in future EPS because an audit qualification indicates that the auditors have serious concerns about the viability of the business or the quality of its earnings. They explained the "unexpected" insignificant result as a function of their sample: The companies in their sample were the ones that survived after having received a qualified opinion.

Abarbanell and Bushee also investigated whether analyst forecast revisions indicate that analysts use these signals to update their earnings forecasts. They found that analysts update their forecasts on the basis of the implications of gross margin, effective tax rate, and labor force but apparently ignore information in inventory. In addition, the authors showed that analysts tend to underreact to the information contained in these signals. Abarbanell and Bushee (1998) showed that by using the information in these fundamental signals they could predict future earnings changes better than analysts or investors.

5. Earnings Management

Earnings management is

> the purposeful intervention in the external financial reporting process, with the intent of obtaining some private gain (as opposed to, say, merely facilitating the neutral operation of the process). (Schipper 1989, p. 92)

Earnings management occurs

> when managers use judgment in financial reporting and in structuring transactions to alter financial reports to either mislead some stakeholders about the underlying economic performance of the company or to influence contractual outcomes that depend on reported accounting numbers. (Healy and Wahlen 1999, p. 368)

Given these definitions of earnings management and our definition of earnings quality—that earnings reflect current performance, that earnings data are useful for predicting future performance, and that the earnings data accurately annuitize intrinsic firm value—clearly, earnings management decreases earnings quality.

Before discussing research into who manages earnings, what they manage, and when, we first take a step back and try to put earnings management in the United States in perspective. How bad is earnings quality in the United States relative to elsewhere in the world? Next, we provide evidence on structuring transactions to manipulate earnings and discuss managing earnings by managing accruals. Finally, we provide evidence from research that has investigated companies' incentives to engage in earnings management. To identify when managers face strong incentives to engage in earnings management requires close scrutiny of the financials by the analyst.

Global Earnings Quality

The financial reporting system in the United States is based on more rules and has greater regulatory and informal monitoring structures than the systems in most other countries. But do these systems and structures result in less earnings management? Several studies have investigated this issue.

Leuz, Nanda, and Wysocki (2003) developed an earnings management score to measure earnings management in various countries. Their aggregate score uses four measures of earnings management: (1) the volatility of earnings relative to the volatility of cash flows, (2) the correlation between cash flows and accruals, (3) the extent of discretion in accruals based on the absolute magnitude of accruals relative to the absolute value of cash flows, and (4) the extent of loss avoidance. A high aggregate score implies "high" earnings management. **Figure 5.1** shows the aggregate score for various countries. The United States ranked as the country with the least amount of earnings management. Leuz et al. also showed that earnings management scores are lower in countries with large stock markets, dispersed ownership, strong investor rights, and strong legal enforcements (i.e., the United States, Australia, and the United Kingdom).

Figure 5.1.   Earnings Management around the World

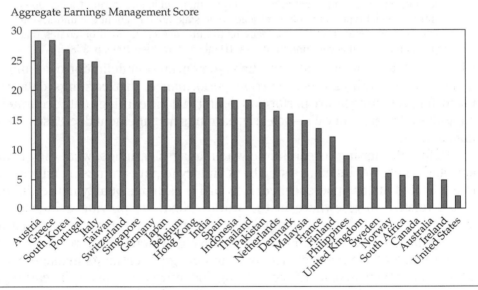

Source: Leuz, Nanda, and Wysocki (2003).

In a related vein, Hung (2000) found that countries with more accrual-related accounting standards have more useful (i.e., value-relevant) earnings when the country has strong shareholder protection (as in the United States). If earnings are more value relevant when accruals are used in the proper manner (i.e., to reduce mismatching problems in cash flows) and less value relevant when accruals are used to manipulate earnings, then an implication of Hung's results is that the United States is likely to experience less earnings management than other economies.

Another approach to investigating the quality of financial reporting in the United States versus elsewhere is through the Form 20-F reconciliations mandated by the U.S. Securities and Exchange Commission (SEC). Foreign companies listing American Depositary Receipts in the United States are required to reconcile their financial statements—based on their domestic generally accepted accounting principles—to U.S. GAAP. The reconciliation components can provide insight into which accounting system elicits earnings information that is the more relevant to investors. Amir, Harris, and Venuti (1993) documented that U.S. GAAP earnings are more value relevant to investors than a company's domestic GAAP earnings. Their results suggest that financial statement quality is generally higher in the United States than elsewhere (see also Barth and Clinch 1996).

Note that the studies we discuss in the remainder of this chapter primarily used U.S. data. Thus, the results may well represent a lower bound on the extent of earnings management in other countries.

Manipulation of Real Transactions

Earnings are composed of cash flows and accruals, and the manipulation of *either* component will affect the earnings number. A manager can take real economic actions that affect cash flows. Examples are cutting research and development (R&D) expenditures and boosting sales by offering products at a discount. The manipulation of real transactions is not a GAAP violation as long as the company properly accounts for the transaction. And these actions generally do not result in a qualified audit opinion or an enforcement action by the SEC. Nonetheless, such actions can have a significant impact on earnings quality and devastating effects on the company's future performance, and the transactions are a form of earnings management.

Using publicly available data to document the extent to which companies engage in real transactions to manipulate earnings is difficult. Observing that a company enters into a transaction that receives favorable accounting treatment is not evidence that the company entered into the transaction just because of its accounting consequences. To show that a company engaged in a transaction purely for accounting purposes, one must know what the company would have or should have or could have done as an alternative.

Several papers have provided compelling evidence about the manipulation of real transactions. Imhoff and Thomas (1988) documented that the use of capital leases dropped sharply after the effective date of Statement of Financial Accounting Standards (SFAS) No. 13, *Accounting for Leases* (FASB 1976), which mandated capitalization for leases with particular terms.[19] Significant substitution into operating leases occurred. Hand (1989) found that companies undertake debt-to-equity swaps to mitigate what would be

---

[19]FASB statements can be found at www.fasb.org/st/.

an unexpected and transitory decline in earnings per share (EPS). Bartov (1993) showed that companies time asset sales to smooth intertemporal earnings changes and also to prevent debt covenant restrictions. Dechow and Sloan (1991) showed that R&D-intensive companies are more likely to cut R&D expenditures just before the chief executive officer's retirement, and Bushee (1998) showed that companies that have little institutional ownership are more likely to cut R&D when earnings are abnormally low.[20] None of these actions violate GAAP, but they certainly affect earnings quality.

Accrual Manipulation

The second way for managers to produce a desired earnings number is to manage accruals. In this method, the company does not change its activities but, rather, opportunistically reports income for an existing activity. Examples that increase income are reducing the allowance for doubtful accounts, capitalizing rather than expensing costs, and avoiding write-offs of assets.

Accruals create the *opportunity* for earnings management because they require managers to make forecasts, estimates, and judgments. The greater the degree of discretion in an accrual, the greater the opportunity for earnings management. Consider the discretion available in the typical accrual adjustments to the following asset and liability accounts.

* *Accounts receivable.* Managers forecast expected product returns and the proportion of customers who will not pay (high discretion).
* *Inventory.* Managers capitalize some costs in inventory and expense other costs as periodic expenses. They forecast expected demand in order to determine future sales prices and whether a write-down is necessary (high discretion).
* *Other current assets.* This account is typically a catchall category for capitalized costs (high discretion).
* *Property, plant, and equipment (PP&E).* Managers capitalize a multitude of costs and depreciate them in arbitrary ways. Managers must also forecast future demand to determine whether an impairment has occurred (high discretion).
* *Accounts or interest payable.* These accounts are amounts owed in dollars to suppliers or debtors (low discretion).

---

[20]We provide further details about the Bushee study in Chapter 6 in the discussion of the role of institutional investors as monitors of earnings quality.

- *Pension liabilities and postretirement benefits.* Managers must forecast the expected return on plan assets, obtain actuarial assumptions on life expectancies, and so forth (high discretion).[21]
- *Long-term debt.* Value is based on the amount received at issuance of long-term debt, and the premium or discount is amortized under specific rules (low discretion).

Accruals management affects only the timing of the recognition of earnings. An overstatement of earnings in one period implies an understatement of earnings in another. For example, an understatement of bad-debt expense in one period (overstated earnings) will result in a write-off of accounts receivable in excess of the allowance (understated earnings) in another. Hence, earnings management strategies based on accruals management are rational only if the expected costs associated with the reversal do not dominate the expected benefits of the initial accruals management. In many cases, the only rational explanation for observed accruals management is managerial optimism: Managers must believe that the accrual reversals will go undetected in future periods when earnings are sufficiently high to absorb the reversals.

Earnings management by opportunistically reporting accruals is not necessarily a violation of GAAP. In many cases, companies can choose among accounting methods. In the spirit of high-quality financial reporting, the right choice is the one that best reflects the economics of the underlying transaction (such as using accelerated depreciation for long-term assets that lose more value early in their service lives). In many cases, however, the company is free to choose among methods without economic justification (e.g., using straight-line depreciation instead of accelerated depreciation).

One result found in many studies is that high accruals, in absolute magnitude, are a potential "red flag" that companies are engaging in earnings management. Dechow, Sloan, and Sweeney (1996) found that companies that were subject to enforcement actions had higher accruals than a control group. Richardson, Tuna, and Wu (2003) found that companies that restate earnings have high accruals in periods before the restatement. Their sample consisted of 338 companies (452 company-year observations) that restated earnings because of accounting abuses. The authors ranked the companies in deciles based on total accruals relative to all companies in the Compustat database. Decile 10 companies had the highest level of accruals (scaled by assets). The results are presented in **Figure 5.2**. A much larger proportion of companies

---

[21]Amir and Benartzi (1998) found that income manipulation affects the selection of the expected rate of return (ERR) on pension assets. They also documented that the allocation of assets between stocks and bonds is a better predictor of future fund performance than the ERR. Amir and Gordon (1996) found that companies manage pension-related estimation parameters, such as discount rates and trends in health care costs, and showed that the management was done to avoid violating debt covenants and to increase the company's bargaining power in plan renegotiations.

Figure 5.2. Frequency of Future Earnings Restatement by Accrual Decile

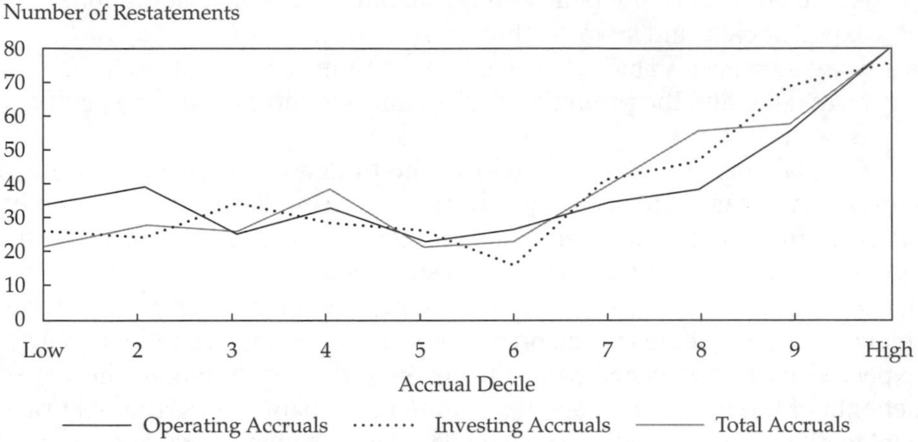

Number of Restatements

Accrual Decile

———— Operating Accruals   ·········· Investing Accruals   ———— Total Accruals

Source: Richardson, Tuna, and Wu (2003).

that subsequently restated earnings had high accruals. The restatements were probably reversing prior overstated accruals.

Our analysis of SEC Accounting and Auditing Enforcement Release (AAER) No. 1 through AAER No. 1745 provides evidence as to which specific accounts are managed. We focused on releases that involved manipulations of annual financial statements and identified 294 separate companies that had manipulated 426 different accounts. **Figure 5.3** summarizes the accounts that the SEC most frequently alleged were manipulated.

Overstatement of revenues is the most common type of earnings management; 70 percent of the cases involved overstated revenue.[22] Further analysis of the revenue overstatements highlights that the SEC is concerned about revenue recognition even if the overstatement of revenue does not affect bottom-line earnings. Some companies are judged on revenue growth, which creates incentives for the companies to manage revenues. One example of boosting revenues without boosting the bottom line is the reporting of barter advertising revenue on a gross basis. The Emerging Issues Task Force (EITF) recently took action to limit when companies can report advertising barter

---

[22]A study by the SEC involving 38 enforcement releases indicated that common revenue recognition problems include recognizing revenue on consignment sales, sales to related parties, bill-and-hold transactions, sales in which ownership had not passed to the customer, shipments not ordered by customers, and nonqualifying barter transactions. Other overstatements related to fictitious sales and delayed recognition of returns. See www.pobauditpanel.org/downloads/appendixf.pdf.

Figure 5.3.   Types and Frequency of Earnings Manipulations

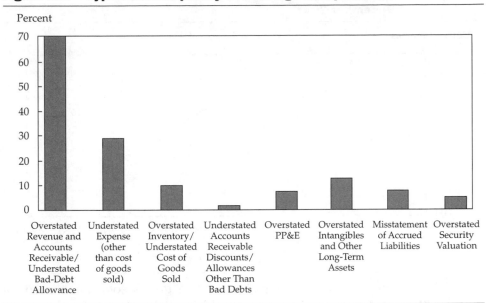

Percent

Note: Based on 294 AAERs that involved the manipulation of 426 different accounts.

transactions on a gross basis (EITF Issue No. 99-17, *Accounting for Advertising Barter Transactions*). Their action was concurrent with the SEC's expressing concerns about these transactions. Another example is Qwest Communications International's accounting for bandwidth swaps so as to allow the company to show continued sales growth.[23] Subsequent restatements of the revenue recognition had no effect on bottom-line earnings.

Figure 5.3 shows that capitalizing costs as long-term assets or overstating PP&E occurred in about 20 percent of the companies. This observation is consistent with Richardson, Sloan, Soliman, and Tuna's (2003) proposition that long-term operating asset and liability accounts (such as PP&E and long-term receivables) are subject to manipulation, despite claims by some that current accruals are easier to manipulate. Richardson et al. suggested that a growing gap between earnings and free cash flow (FCF) can be viewed as a red flag about earnings quality. **Figure 5.4** shows the earnings-to-FCF gap for WorldCom from the early 1990s through 2001. The plot illustrates a growing gap through the year 2000, which investors now know was the result of capitalizing rather than expensing current costs.

---

[23]See, AAER No. 1879 at www.sec.gov/divisions/enforce/friactions.shtml.

Figure 5.4. WorldCom Earnings and Free Cash Flows, December 1992–December 2001

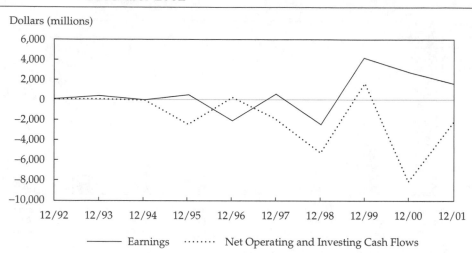

Understating expenses (other than cost of goods sold) accounted for almost 30 percent of the allegations (see Figure 5.3); overstating inventory (and understating cost of goods sold) accounted for approximately 10 percent. The SEC alleged in approximately 8 percent of the cases that the companies were creating hidden reserves. These cases involved the overstatement of liabilities, such as a restructuring accrual, to be drawn down in future periods to boost operating performance.

Nelson, Elliott, and Tarpley (2003) provided a different perspective on the various accounts most frequently managed. Their sample consisted of 515 attempts at earnings management obtained from a survey of 253 experienced auditors from one of the Big Five accounting firms. They reported the categories of earnings management attempts shown in **Table 5.1**.

Their analysis indicates that 272 of 515 (53 percent) of the earnings management attempts were made to increase income and that the auditor adjusted for these income-increasing attempts in 52 percent of the cases. The most common type of earnings management attempt was an attempt to adjust an expense or loss through the manipulation of reserves or through the capitalization or deferral of costs (269 cases). These attempts include recording inappropriate reserves for such items as restructuring charges, provisions for loan losses, write-offs of inventory, and asset impairments. These items are generally classified as "special items" in the income statement, and the measurement of the charge involves significant estimation and judgment, which creates opportunities for earnings management.

Table 5.1. Number of Earnings Management Attempts and the Percentage Adjusted by Auditor

Approach	Total Attempts	Attempt to Increase Income	Percent of All Attempts Adjusted by Auditor	Percent of Increase Attempts Adjusted by Auditor
Attempt to adjust an expense or other recorded loss	269	133	42%	48%
Attempt to adjust revenue or other recorded gain	114	86	56%	62%
Business combination	67	12	40%	67%
Other approaches	65	41	34%	41%
Total/Percent adjusted	515	272	44%	52%

Source: Table 1 of Nelson, Elliott, and Tarpley (2003).

In the Nelson et al. sample, the second most common type of earnings management attempt was adjusting revenue or other gains (114 attempts). The cases involved cutoff manipulation (booking sales after the fiscal year-end), recording bill-and-hold sales, and recording sales with a right of return. Of these attempts, 86 of 114 (75 percent) would have increased income, and the auditor required an adjustment in 62 percent of the cases.

The results of SEC enforcement actions and audited earnings management attempts suggest that an analyst should carefully scrutinize accounts receivable (including bad-debt allowances), inventory, capitalized costs for PP&E, intangible assets (such as software development), and liabilities that are difficult to estimate. All these accounts require management to make forecasts and estimates, and the company can use this discretion to boost current or future earnings.

Beyond focusing on the *level* of specific accruals, how can an analyst detect earnings management? Accounting research has put considerable effort into producing models to identify legitimate ("nondiscretionary") accruals versus managed ("discretionary") components. A common model used to detect discretionary accruals or earnings management is the Jones (1991) model. Using time-series data for a company, this model estimates expected accruals as follows:[24]

$$\text{Accruals}_t = \alpha + \beta_1 (\Delta \text{Revenue}) + \beta_2 (\text{PP\&E}) + \epsilon_t. \tag{5.1}$$

---

[24]Some papers (e.g., DeFond and Jiambalvo 1994) estimated this model for a sample of companies in a single industry rather than for a single company across time periods. Such cross-sectional estimation assumes that the relationships among revenues and PP&E and accruals are relatively stable within the group of companies.

All the variables in this model are scaled by assets. Expected accruals, which are assumed to be nondiscretionary accruals, are equal to $\alpha + \beta_1(\Delta\text{Revenue}_j) + \beta_2(\text{PP\&E}_j)$, where α, β_1, and β_2 are estimates from the regression (Equation 5.1). Discretionary accruals are equal to ϵ, the residual from the regression.[25]

The main criticism of this model is that it does not control for growth. If accruals do not move one for one with sales and PP&E as these variables grow, the estimate of discretionary accruals will be measured with error. Our reason for including the model here is that it highlights the importance of appropriate benchmarks for evaluating accruals. When examining accruals, analysts need to consider changes in fundamental variables, such as revenues and long-lived assets, that reflect changes in the underlying operations of the company; these fundamental changes clearly have an impact on nondiscretionary accruals. A company's change in accruals relative to changes for other companies in the same industry is also an important consideration. Other companies provide a useful benchmark for pinpointing what is nondiscretionary.

Identifying the discretionary component of accruals by using regression analysis can be difficult in practice. In many circumstances that an analyst faces, focusing on the level of *total accruals* is a simple and easy way to identify discretionary accruals. Total accruals and discretionary accruals are highly positively correlated. Dechow, Richardson, and Tuna (2003) showed that the correlation between estimated discretionary accruals (from accrual models) and total accruals is higher than 80 percent.

Incentives for Earnings Management

Earnings management requires opportunity and motive. In this section, we analyze situations that create *motives* for earnings management. By understanding when companies have incentives to manage earnings, readers of financial statements can assess when a company is likely to engage in such behavior. Note that the earnings management decision represents a trade-off between costs and benefits. This discussion focuses on the benefits of earnings management.

Dechow, Sloan, and Sweeney (1996) studied 92 AAERs that accused companies of engaging in earnings manipulation between 1978 and 1990. Thirty-nine of the AAERs provided at least one explanation for the earnings management; the remaining fifty-three AAERs provided no explanation.

---

[25] Dechow, Sloan, and Sweeney (1995) suggested the following "modification" to the original Jones model. If manipulation is predicted to occur in year j, then discretionary accruals in that year are calculated as $\text{Accruals}_j - [\alpha + \beta_1(\Delta\text{Revenue}_j - \Delta\text{Accounts receivable}_j) + \beta_2(\text{PP\&E}_j)]$. This modification increases the power of the model to detect revenue overstatements because it does not assume, as the original Jones model did, that all changes in revenue are nondiscretionary.

Table 5.2. Motivations for the Manipulation of Earnings

Motivation	Number
Issue securities at higher prices	22
Report upwardly trending EPS	11
Increase the size of earnings-based bonuses	7
Profit from insider trading	6
Other	3
Total[a]	49

[a]Eight AAERs provided more than one explanation.

Table 5.2 contains the results of their study. They suggested that three main factors create incentives for earnings management. First, capital market transactions are associated with earnings management. In more than half of the cases examined, managers manipulated earnings either to issue securities at higher prices or to profit from insider trading. Second, the desire to report upwardly trending earnings per share, presumably to meet the expectations of analysts and investors, is a motivation for engaging in earnings management. Third, contractual incentives are motives for earnings management— for example, manipulating earnings to increase the size of earnings-based bonuses. The remainder of this chapter discusses empirical research into each of these incentives.

Capital Market Incentives. Research has documented the existence of earnings management in connection with

- seasoned equity offerings,
- initial public offerings,
- mergers and management buyouts, and
- insider equity transactions.

The incentive in these instances is to affect the company's stock price. Stock is currency in these transactions, and price matters. Moreover, short-term stock price matters. Even if managers know that the effects of the earnings management will eventually reverse, they have incentives to manage earnings in the current period to manipulate the transaction price. The greater stock price associated with the managed earnings, even if only in the short run, reduces the cost of acquiring new capital or the effective price of an acquisition, or it increases the manager's personal wealth. (An underlying assumption of this research is that investors do not rationally anticipate the earnings management. If they did, managers would have no reason to engage in the behavior and bear the costs associated with potentially getting caught.)

An important aspect that the research into capital market incentives for earnings management highlights is that earnings management may involve artificially *decreasing* instead of artificially increasing earnings. Management buyouts are an example of a capital market transaction that provides incentives for a manager to manage earnings in order to decrease the company's stock price—at least in the short run—and reduce the buyout price.

■ *Seasoned equity offerings.* SEOs provide an incentive for companies to manage earnings to increase stock prices prior to the offerings. And research findings are consistent with the intuition that some companies engage in earnings management prior to SEOs (Rangan 1998; Teoh, Welch, and Wong 1998b). **Figure 5.5** shows returns for four groups of companies classified by their pre-issue levels of discretionary current accruals (DCA) from Teoh, Welch, and Wong (1998b).[26] Companies were classified into quartiles based on discretionary current accruals in the fiscal year prior to the offering. The

Figure 5.5.   Stock Returns Following SEOs

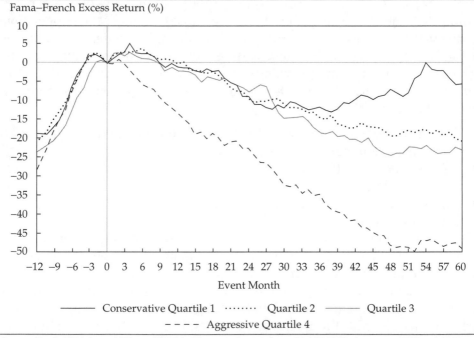

Source: Teoh, Welch, and Wong (1998b). The sample consists of 1,248 SEOs between 1970 and 1989.

[26]The authors considered current assets and liabilities (excluding the current portion of long-term debt) to be easier to manipulate than long-term accruals. Thus, their measure of discretionary accruals was changes in current accrual assets and current accrual liabilities that were not related to changes in sales and PP&E, where the estimated relationships between the accruals and the other measures were assumed constant within an industry.

graphed returns are the logged cumulative sum of monthly portfolio excess returns relative to the Fama–French (1993) model, normalized so that the offering month return is zero.[27]

Figure 5.5 shows two important patterns. First, all the companies making SEOs had increasing returns prior to the offering. The similar return performance across the groups suggests that investors did not recognize any difference in the quality of earnings among the four groups prior to the offering. This result is important because the companies were classified by using publicly available data. Thus, investors could have identified the aggressive and conservative companies as Teoh, Welch, and Wong did. Second, the most aggressive earnings managers experienced the worst underperformance after the SEO. Eventually, the low quality of earnings for the Aggressive Quartile 4 portfolio was revealed, probably as the discretionary accruals were reversed.

Teoh, Welch, and Wong (1998b) interpreted the observed patterns as evidence that companies manage earnings through accruals prior to an SEO and that the market is fooled by the earnings management. Investors overreact to the managed earnings and are subsequently "disappointed" by poor earnings performance when the accruals reverse. Rangan supported these findings. Shivakumar (2000), however, argued that these tests are misspecified; he believed that investors rationally anticipate the earnings management around an SEO and "undo" its effects. An alternative explanation for the apparent overreaction to earnings prior to an SEO and the subsequent disappointment is that the high-accrual companies, which the studies identified as earnings managers, are really high-growth companies, for which the models of accruals do not fit the data well. High-growth companies are likely to have the most optimistic forecasts of future growth, and the market is subsequently disappointed when that growth is not realized. In a follow-up paper, Teoh and Wong (2002) found that discretionary accruals in the offering year predict analysts' errors in annual earnings forecasts for as many as four fiscal years after the new issue. The discretionary accruals also predict the analysts' errors in five-year growth forecasts made in the offering year. Analysts and investors appear to suffer from similar biases.

■ *Initial public offerings.* A company's initial public offering (IPO) also provides incentives for earnings management, and the opportunity may be even greater than the opportunities around an SEO. IPOs typically have a shorter operating history than SEOs. Even for old companies, the amount of publicly available historical financial information is smaller for IPOs than for SEOs. Thus, it is more difficult for market participants to estimate for IPOs the nondiscretionary or unmanaged portion of accruals and the managed

---

[27]The Fama–French classic model of expected returns consists of three factors: (1) the market return (return on a value-weighted market index less a risk-free rate of return), (2) company size (small minus large), and (3) company book-to-market value (low minus high).

portion. Because the probability of fooling investors is greater with IPOs, the expected benefits of managing earnings are greater and are more likely to outweigh the costs.

As for SEOs, research evidence consistently indicates that companies manage earnings by using discretionary accruals prior to IPOs. The accruals eventually reverse, however, which explains (at least in part) the long-run underperformance of IPOs (Teoh, Welch, and Wong 1998a; Teoh, Wong, and Rao 1998; DuCharme, Malatesta, and Sefcik 2001). Aharony, Lin, and Loeb (1993), however, did not find much evidence that IPO issuers make unusual accounting choices that would be consistent with earnings management.

■ *Mergers and management buyouts.* Around a merger, both the acquirer and the target have incentives to manage earnings to increase stock prices, and evidence shows that both parties do. Erickson and Wang (1999) found evidence consistent with income-increasing earnings management by acquiring companies in stock-for-stock mergers between 1985 and 1990. Easterwood (1998) found evidence that takeover targets—primarily targets of hostile takeovers—use discretionary accruals to inflate earnings (compared with the discretionary accruals by nontarget companies) during the quarters immediately preceding and following a takeover attempt. Christie and Zimmerman (1994) also showed that targets more frequently select income-increasing accounting methods than do nontargets for depreciation, inventory, and investment tax credits. The authors suggested that efficiency, however, rather than opportunism is the primary driver in the accounting choice. The evidence is not conflicting: Companies may be more likely to manage discretionary accruals, which may go unnoticed, than to manage a publicized accounting choice, such as its depreciation method, which investors can easily observe.

In a management buyout, in contrast to a takeover, managers have incentives to minimize the purchase price, potentially through income-decreasing earnings management that will negatively affect the company's stock price. Two papers on management buyouts during the 1980s provided evidence of earnings management prior to buyouts. Perry and Williams (1994) found abnormal negative behavior of discretionary accruals for buyout companies in the year before managers announced their buyout intentions. Wu (1997) reported that earnings changes are significantly smaller than industry median changes for buyout companies in the year preceding the buyout. DeAngelo (1986), however, did not find evidence of accrual management for management buyouts during the 1973–82 period. DeAngelo's findings may be a result of the different time period examined, the different research method used, or the use of a less powerful earnings management proxy.

■ *Insider equity transactions*. Insiders have incentives to increase earnings to artificially inflate stock prices, even if only in the short run, around the time they anticipate selling shares. Beneish and Vargus (2002) provided two kinds of evidence related to earnings management at the time of insider equity transactions. First, they documented that it exists. When income-increasing accruals occurred contemporaneously with unusual insider trading activity, the accrual-related earnings had lower persistence to the one-year-ahead accounting period. The lower persistence was at least partly a result of accruals management. Second, they documented that a hypothetical long–short trading strategy that takes positions based on the *direction* of companies' accruals and contemporaneous insider trading activity earns positive hedge returns. This evidence does not suggest that investors can earn abnormal returns by forming portfolios on the basis of insider trades and accruals; investors do not have information about a contemporaneous insider trade until after the trade is made. The evidence does suggest, however, that public information about insider trading activity, which is disclosed on or before the 10th day of the month after the event, can help analysts and investors assess the probability that the accruals prior to the insider's sale or purchase were likely to have been managed.

■ *Summary*. The key point of this section is that *any* event that involves stock being purchased or sold or otherwise used as currency provides managers with incentives to manage earnings to influence investor perception of firm value. We pointed out that companies that are issuing new financing and that also have high accruals are the most overvalued by investors. Whether this overvaluation stems from earnings management or from investors' misunderstanding of the growth potential of high-accrual companies is an open question. In either case, analysts should understand that these companies are likely to have low-quality earnings that should be scrutinized carefully.

Managing Earnings to Forecasts and Other Targets. Identifying the targets toward which companies manage earnings can help identify companies that are likely candidates for managing earnings. Companies that report earnings that barely meet or beat a target may have managed the earnings to do so.

The literature related to earnings targets is extensive and varied. One target that has been considered is simply zero. This research claims that companies do not want to report negative earnings and will manage earnings just enough to get over the zero threshold. In other words, managers believe there is a stigma to reporting negative earnings. Reporting positive $0.01 per share may be worse than reporting positive $0.02, but reporting –$0.01 is *significantly* worse than reporting $0.00.

Hayn (1995) and Burgstahler and Dichev (1997b) showed that the frequency with which companies report earnings that are barely less than zero is lower than the frequency with which companies report earnings just greater than zero. The histogram of earnings observations in **Figure 5.6** illustrates this result. One interpretation of the observed pattern in earnings realizations is that earnings that are just above the target are managed.

Although the pattern in Figure 5.6 is striking, it is not *a priori* evidence of earnings management. In fact, researchers who have attempted to verify that the companies with earnings barely over the zero threshold were managing earnings have not been able to do so by using statistical models of discretionary accruals. Dechow, Richardson, and Tuna (2003) suggested other potential explanations for the observed pattern. For example, managers and employees may simply work harder to improve company performance when they are close to the zero threshold. And sample selection biases could also play a role. Beaver, McNichols, and Nelson (2003) also proposed alternative explanations for the pattern. They claimed that asymmetrical tax treatment of profits and losses and conservatism related to the reporting of special items can cause the kink at zero. So, although certainly not all companies with earnings just over the zero threshold have managed earnings to get there, low but positive earnings are a potential red flag for earnings management.

Figure 5.6.   Distribution of Earnings Scaled by Market Value (Truncated), Data for 1988–2000

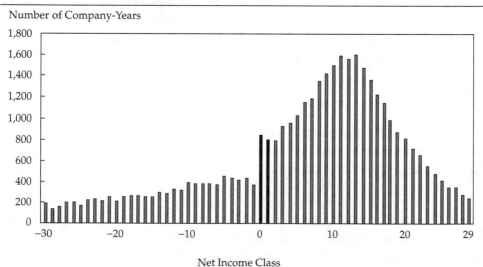

Notes: The sample was 47,847 company-years. Bolded classes represent income/market value that is just above zero
Source: Dechow, Richardson, and Tuna (2003). Burgstahler and Dichev (1997b) and Hayn (1995) contain similar figures.

Researchers also have investigated whether companies manage earnings to meet analysts' consensus forecasts. **Figure 5.7** provides a plot of forecast errors, which represent the difference between the actual earnings realization and the consensus forecast, for annual forecasts (the figure is similar when quarterly data were used). A positive forecast error indicates that the actual earnings beat the forecast. The plot reveals an obvious pattern: A larger-than-expected number of companies meet or barely beat analysts' forecasts. There are more small positive forecast errors than small negative forecast errors. This pattern would not be expected if analysts were equally likely to overestimate or underestimate earnings and if companies did not engage in earnings manipulation to exceed a target.

Again, the observed pattern in forecast errors is suggestive (but not conclusive) that companies engage in earnings management to meet or beat forecasts. The question of whether companies manage earnings to meet analysts' forecasts is complicated, however, because the target (unlike the number zero) is not exogenous. A company might meet analysts' forecasts because analysts are good at forecasting earnings, because the company's earnings are easy to forecast, or because managers provide "guidance" to analysts about expected earnings. Nonetheless, the fact that a company consistently just meets the consensus forecast is a potential red flag that earnings quality is low.

Figure 5.7. Distribution of Analyst Forecast Errors

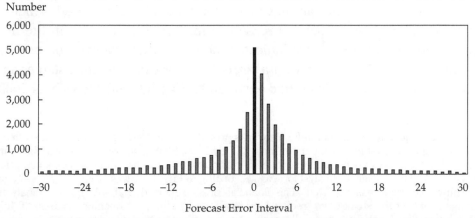

Notes: The distribution is as reported in I/B/E/S. The interval width is 1 cent; for example, the number at −30 includes all company-years when the consensus forecast was missed by 30 cents.

Source: Dechow, Richardson, and Tuna (2001).

This red flag is especially relevant for high-growth companies. The stock prices of these companies are particularly hard hit by investors when the companies subsequently miss the consensus forecast (Skinner and Sloan 2002). Not every company that barely meets its forecast, however, is equally likely to have a precipitous stock price decline, which the Skinner and Sloan study called an earnings "torpedo."[28] Torpedoes are more likely when a company does not meet revenue growth expectations but still manages to meet earnings expectations. Such a company is potentially sacrificing future earnings to boost current earnings by understating expenses.

Kasznik (1999) found, in a related study, that companies manage earnings toward their own annual earnings forecasts. Kasznik documented abnormally high positive discretionary accruals when earnings would otherwise have been below management forecasts. He interpreted this finding as evidence that managers manage reported earnings toward their own forecasts, but he also recognized that the abnormal level of discretionary accruals might have motivated the issuance of the forecast or that the two could have been simultaneously determined as part of an overall reporting strategy.

A final issue to consider when thinking about how targets provide incentives for earnings management, and thus affect earnings quality, is why companies care about meeting targets. Trying to meet targets solely through earnings manipulation is not rational if investors assume that earnings that barely meet or beat a target are managed. In that case, rational investors will ascribe less value to the earnings that are assumed to be managed, which in turn means managers have no reason to manage the earnings in the first place. Some recent evidence indicates, however, that investors do not discount earnings that are just over a target (see, for example, Burgstahler and Eames 2003; Bartov, Givoly, and Hayn 2002; Kasznik and McNichols 2002;

---

[28]The earnings announcement of F5 Networks provides an interesting example of the effects of missing an analyst forecast. On Tuesday, 25 July 2000, F5 announced for the first time that it would record tax expense and that its EPS (after taxes) would be 17 cents. The stock price was $42.50. The consensus analyst forecast, according to First Call, was 18 cents, and a –1 cent earnings surprise was reported. The financial press reported that missing the analysts' consensus sent the stock price "reeling" in after-hours trading; the opening price on 26 July was below $39. That day, First Call announced that it had aggregated analysts' estimates of pretax and post-tax earnings for F5 in error. The new pretax estimate was 19 cents, and the after-tax average was 14 cents. As a result, the company beat the consensus by 3 cents. Its share price rose to $46. In this example, investors appear to have been reacting more to whether the company beat the consensus than the fact that it had an EPS of 17 cents.

Matsumoto 2002; Dhaliwal, Gleason, and Mills 2002; Abarbanell and Lehavy 2003).[29] The evidence suggests that there are some real benefits to meeting forecasts and that, whether the benefits are real or perceived, managers attribute value to meeting forecasts.

Contracting Incentives for Earnings Management. Various types of contracting arrangements provide companies with a direct incentive to manage earnings. Debt contracts, compensation contracts, and tax regulations or other regulations—which we will loosely refer to as "contracts"—may contain provisions that are a function of GAAP earnings and thus provide incentives for earnings management. A company's regulatory environment also can contain earnings management incentives—not only because some regulations, such as capital requirements, are explicitly based on earnings but also because a company's profitability may be associated with regulatory pressure.

A significant distinction of contract-based incentives for earnings management is that the motivation is obvious. The contract specifies a particular earnings-based number the company must meet to avoid costs or to gain some benefit. The incentive to manage earnings is direct; no assumptions or predictions are needed about who is rational and what managers, investors, or contracting parties believe about the rationality of the other parties. If the contracting parties detect or undo the manipulation, it will not matter.

Consider capital regulations as an example. Banks that violate capital requirements incur both out-of-pocket and opportunity costs. For a significantly undercapitalized bank, regulators can require recapitalization or can force the institution into conservatorship or receivership. Banks that fail to meet minimum capital requirements must submit a comprehensive capital restoration plan to regulators, which is costly to prepare and implement. In addition, during the time that a bank is undercapitalized, its regulators can restrict dividends and management fees. The regulators can also exercise control over the bank's operations by placing limits on branching, expansion, and new services. Even for banks with capital above the minimum requirement, greater capital creates a competitive advantage. Well-capitalized institutions face fewer regulatory constraints on operations than poorly capitalized institutions, enjoy more timely approval for expansion and growth from federal banking agencies, and pay lower Federal Deposit Insurance

---

[29] One explanation for the fact that investors do not discount earnings that are just over a target is that it takes time for them to distinguish manipulators from nonmanipulators. Balsam, Bartov, and Marquardt (2002) investigated the stock price reactions to 10-Q filings and the use of discretionary accruals to meet or just beat analyst forecasts. Companies that met a forecast by using discretionary accruals had a negative stock price reaction at the 10-Q filing date, which is presumably when the market recognizes the larger-than-expected accruals.

Corporation premiums.[30] Thus, even if one assumes that bank regulators are perfectly able to anticipate and detect earnings management and, therefore, understand that capital is above the requirement only because earnings are of low quality, banks still have incentives to manage earnings to be above the requirement in order to avoid regulatory costs that are a function of strict capital requirements.

When thinking about the incentives that a contracting arrangement provides for earnings management, analysts need to consider the specific *nature* of the arrangement and the *type* of incentives it provides. Not all contracting arrangements provide incentives to *maximize* reported earnings. For example, although for most financial institutions regulatory capital constraints provide incentives to inflate earnings to meet the constraint, institutions with capital that is significantly below the requirement may have incentives to engage in behavior that creates volatility; they are hoping for a big upside realization while not viewing a big downside realization as costly. That is, the company may try to maximize the value of the "put option" to the federal government that results from the existence of deposit insurance by increasing earnings volatility (see Ronn and Verma 1986). Contracts with creditors often include multiple covenants, and a company may have to manage particular components of earnings to meet all the covenants. As for taxes, companies have incentives to manipulate components of *taxable* income (not GAAP income), which often requires manipulation of real transactions—such as selling certain securities that are in a gain or loss position—rather than accruals management. Earnings management incentives derived from compensation contracts can be particularly complex. Bonus schemes, for example, can have a minimum threshold that must be met followed by a range over which the bonus is a linear function of earnings up to a predetermined maximum. Such nonlinearities in the relationship between compensation and earnings affect a manager's incentives to manage earnings. And political costs often cause incentives for companies to manage earnings downward to look less profitable and more in need of "subsidies" or favorable antitrust decisions, union concessions, or import relief. In summary, understanding which companies have direct incentives to manage earnings is important because of contracting relationships and what the contract provides an incentive to do.

■ *Capital/regulatory constraints.* In general, the evidence is strong that financial institutions manage earnings to meet or beat regulatory capital requirements. The bulk of this research focuses on management of loan-loss provisions or insurance reserves in financial institutions (see, e.g., Ahmed,

---

[30]See the discussions of costs associated with violating bank capital requirements in Rose (1996) and Moyer (1990).

Takeda, and Thomas 1999; Beatty, Chamberlain, and Magliolo 1996), primarily because researchers can confidently measure the discretionary component of accruals. They can observe *ex post* whether reserves were too high or too low. Evidence about other accounts, such as the valuation allowance against deferred tax assets (Schrand and Wong 2003), is more limited. All of the research reaches the same conclusion: Capital requirements provide strong incentives for earnings management. The costs of not meeting the requirement are significant, and all earnings, managed or not, help the institution meet the requirement.

The research about earnings management to meet capital and regulatory requirements clearly makes an important point: Although managing capital is important, companies also have other incentives for managing earnings and the various incentives may not all lead to the same optimal reporting strategy. Companies may want to manage regulatory capital, GAAP earnings, and taxable income simultaneously (see, for example, Collins, Shackelford, and Wahlen 1995; Chen and Daley 1996). The ultimate earnings management decision will represent a trade-off between the costs and the benefits associated with all the earnings management incentives.

■ *Debt covenants.* Debt contracts commonly contain covenants based on accounting numbers or ratios. DeAngelo, DeAngelo, and Skinner (1994) and Sweeney (1994) found somewhat conflicting evidence on earnings management related to debt covenants. Both papers predicted that companies would engage in income-increasing behavior to avoid costly violation of debt covenants. DeAngelo et al., however, did not find evidence of such behavior for a sample of "financially troubled" companies (defined as those that reported at least three annual losses and reduced cash dividends in the six-year period of 1980–1985). The accrual behavior of the companies with binding covenants and those with nonbinding covenants was not significantly different. DeAngelo et al. provided some evidence that the more troubled companies with binding constraints had more negative accruals, but the accruals were related to inventory write-offs, which are probably a result of real troubles, not discretionary decisions.

In contrast, Sweeney found evidence that as companies approach violation of their debt covenants, they respond with more income-increasing accounting changes. And Dichev and Skinner (2002) revealed unusual patterns in reported current ratios and net worth around the thresholds for these variables set in *private* debt agreements.

Jaggi and Lee (2002) offered evidence that potentially reconciles the conflicting results. They found that some financially distressed companies use income-increasing discretionary accruals and some use income-decreasing discretionary accruals to manage earnings. They observed income-decreasing accruals by companies that were not able to obtain waivers of the debt covenants and that were forced to renegotiate or restructure their debt, but they observed income-increasing accruals by companies that were able to obtain debt waivers.

One caveat about all of this research is that measuring discretionary accruals by using statistical models for companies in financial distress is difficult because the estimated model parameters may not be representative of the relationships within a particular distressed company or be stable through time.

■ *Executive compensation contracts.* A question that has been researched quite extensively is whether managers manipulate accruals to maximize earnings-based bonuses. Initial evidence by Healy (1985) supported this claim. He noted that earnings-based bonus plans frequently have upper and lower bounds. When earnings are below the lower bound, no bonus is awarded; when earnings are above the upper bound, no additional bonus is paid; and when earnings are between the bounds, the bonus is a function of earnings. For such arrangements, Healy predicted that managers had an incentive to increase earnings in order to increase the bonus only when unmanaged earnings were between the bounds. When unmanaged earnings were below the lower bound or above the upper bound, managers had an incentive to decrease earnings and "reserve" them for future periods when earnings were within the bonus range. His evidence is consistent with this prediction for a sample of 1,527 company-year observations for 1930–1980.

More recent research using different sample periods has had difficulty replicating Healy's findings. For example, Gaver, Gaver, and Austin (1995) investigated bonus plans for 1980–1990 and found that companies with unmanaged earnings above the upper bound used income-decreasing discretionary accruals, which is consistent with Healy's findings. They found, however, that companies with unmanaged earnings below the lower bound used income-increasing discretionary accruals, which is opposite to the results reported by Healy. The results found by Gaver et al. suggest that companies manage earnings to smooth the earnings series rather than to maximize bonuses. Holthausen, Larcker, and Sloan (1995) used a confidential dataset for which the lower and upper bounds of the contract were known. They found evidence of earnings management to decrease earnings and create reserves when earnings were greater than the upper bound but found no evidence that earnings were managed downward when earnings were below the lower bound.

In summary, although it seems intuitive that earnings-based bonuses would provide an incentive to engage in earnings management, recent research has not been able to document this effect or the extent to which it might occur. One explanation for the lack of evidence relates to the research methods: That is, earnings management may exist, but researchers do not have adequate information about the nature of the incentives to design statistically powerful enough tests to detect it. It could be, however, that, despite the intuitive appeal of a link between earnings-based compensation contracts and earnings management, certain forces mitigate the compensation-related incentive. For example, boards of directors may be able to adjust bonuses to exclude "managed" earnings either informally or through formal contract provisions, such as making the bonus a function of only those earnings components that contain little discretion. If so, managing earnings provides no bonus-related benefit.

Also, the fact that early evidence showed a link between bonuses and earnings management whereas later evidence did not suggests that incentives have changed. The incentive to manage earnings to maximize bonuses may have decreased, but it may have been replaced by incentives to manage earnings to influence the stock price and maximize stock-based compensation. The conjecture that managers have incentives to manage earnings related to stock-based compensation is predicated on the assumption that managers believe the managed earnings will be mispriced and the manager will be able to take advantage of the mispricing before it is corrected—either by selling shares or by exercising options. The evidence in Richardson, Tuna, and Wu; Beneish (1999); Cheng and Warfield (2003); and Gao and Shrieves (2002) suggests that earnings management increases with the extent to which managers have stock-based compensation.

■ *Political incentives.* Various studies have argued that governmental and nongovernmental organizations, although not necessarily intended users of financial statements, create incentives for companies to manage reported earnings because they can impose costs on companies that are "too profitable." High profits can bring attention to a company that would otherwise like to stay off the regulatory radar screen. More importantly, high profits may be used as evidence that the company is gouging its customers. Agencies that serve to protect consumer interests may attempt to regulate prices charged by companies that show high profits. Note that the somewhat unusual feature of this political cost argument to explain earnings management is that it predicts that companies will manage earnings *down*.

Many of the studies have looked for earnings management during specific periods when regulatory scrutiny of an industry was high and high profits would invite harmful regulation. For example, evidence indicates that companies in the cable television industry recorded income-decreasing discretionary accruals during periods of U.S. Congressional hearings aimed at regulating cable prices (Key 1997), that chemical companies recorded income-decreasing discretionary accruals when Congress was debating Superfund site legislation (Cahan, Chavis, and Elmendorf 1997), and that companies investigated for antitrust merger violations engaged in earnings management through discretionary accruals to lower "excess" profits because regulators might interpret excess profits as an indication of an anticompetitive environment (Makar, Alam, and Pearson 1998).

Other related studies include that of Jones (1991), who showed that companies record income-decreasing discretionary accruals during import-relief investigations, and Hall and Stammerjohan (1997), who showed that companies manage earnings downward when faced with outstanding litigation with potentially large damage awards. Liberty and Zimmerman (1986) and DeAngelo and DeAngelo (1991), who suggested that managers have incentives to manage earnings downward before labor union negotiations to strengthen their bargaining positions, found mixed results.

An important question related to political cost incentives for earnings management concerns the assumed sophistication of the contracting parties: Is it reasonable to assume that regulatory agencies have access only to publicly available information? Could they not obtain more detailed cost records to determine appropriate regulatory pricing intervention or to assess "excess" profits available for unionized employees or plaintiffs? Assuming that managers believe they can fool a diffuse group of investors with little access to important internal financial information may be plausible. And assuming that Congress, which has access to detailed internal records, will not "undo" earnings manipulation when making decisions may also be plausible (because lower profits provide Congress with a way to justify their political decisions to constituents who are not so well informed). But assuming that managers believe they can fool import-relief investigators, labor union negotiators, and plaintiffs' attorneys is not so plausible. These parties have access to private information and the incentive to carefully undo earnings manipulation. Thus, in these situations, one might question why a manager would believe that any benefit is to be gained by engaging in earnings management. Nonetheless, the evidence suggests that managers do manage earnings for "political" reasons.

■ *Tax incentives.* Studies of incentives for earnings management created by tax codes generally examine changes in accruals or activities around the time of a significant change in tax regulations. Although this approach is a statistically powerful way to test for tax incentives for earnings management, it means that the research findings may not be generalizable to periods that do not include any significant changes in tax regulations. Tax incentives for earnings management may dominate other incentives in periods of significant tax law changes, but they may be less important at other times.

Research studies have documented several significant tax-related events that induced earnings management. Scholes, Wilson, and Wolfson (1992) showed that companies timed revenue and expense recognition to defer income in anticipation of lower tax rates in the mid-1980s. Maydew (1997) found that companies shifted recognition of revenues and expenses to take advantage of significant tax code changes in the Tax Reform Act of 1986—in particular, changes related to the treatment of provisions for net operating losses. He also found that the degree of earnings management was associated with the magnitude of the potential benefits. Boynton, Dobbins, and Plesko (1992) found, by looking at earnings patterns around the initiation of the alternative minimum tax, that earnings management is associated with a company's exposure to the AMT. A somewhat contradictory result is the finding by Scholes et al. (1992) that earnings management exists for large companies but not for small companies. They concluded that the larger companies are more efficient tax planners. Boynton et al., however, found that earnings management is *more* pronounced for small companies (where size was measured by total assets).

The studies cited in this last section all indicate that companies manage the timing of earnings recognition to decrease current-period taxes. But in many cases, earnings manipulation will not affect a company's tax obligation. The company must manage real transactions—adjust its investment, financing, and operating decisions—to manage taxable income. Unlike simply managing the *timing* of earnings recognition associated with existing transactions, this form of earnings management has real cash flow implications, and the benefits of the earnings management must exceed the costs. Nonetheless, evidence indicates that such manipulations occur. For example, Scholes et al. (1990) showed that companies adjusted their security holdings in response to tax code changes specifically related to banks during the mid-1980s.

6. Corporate Governance and Other Monitors

A question that naturally arises in a discussion of earnings management is how companies are able to get away with it. Citations of the U.S. securities markets as the best regulated, most liquid, most efficient markets in the world are too numerous to mention. So, how does the phenomenon of earnings management persist despite the existence of the various monitors—auditors, institutional investors, creditors, boards of directors and their audit committees, and analysts? Do they not see it? Do they see it and ignore it? Why don't they prevent it?

The U.S. Securities and Exchange Commission enforcement actions studied by Dechow, Sloan, and Sweeney (1996), which were described in Chapter 5, provide an overview of the effect of various corporate governance mechanisms in assuring earnings quality. The SEC identifies companies that violate U.S. generally accepted accounting principles (GAAP) in a number of ways. It gets tips from insiders, it does its own analyses, and it follows up on companies that voluntarily restate earnings because of accounting irregularities.

SEC enforcement actions are serious, and the types of manipulation involved are typically the most egregious (e.g., fraudulently increasing sales, recognizing sales before the sales are complete, delaying the write-off of obsolete inventory, capitalizing excessive costs into inventory). Thus, the "enforcement action" sample of companies is at the extreme end of the low-earnings-quality spectrum. If corporate governance plays a prominent role in ensuring earnings quality, then one would expect to see weaker corporate governance in these companies than in the control sample.

Figure 6.1 reports characteristics of the SEC enforcement companies as compared with those of a control sample of nonenforcement companies in 1996. At this time, enforcement companies were less likely than controls to have a Big Six auditor (although this difference is not statistically significant) and were less likely to have an audit committee.[30] They were also less likely to have an independent outside blockholder (such as an institutional investor) that had an incentive to monitor the company. And their boards of directors were less independent. The enforcement companies more often

---

[30] The time of the study is prior to the New York Stock Exchange mandate that all listed companies have an audit committee.

Figure 6.1.   Governance Structure for Companies that Violated GAAP vs. Control Group, 1996

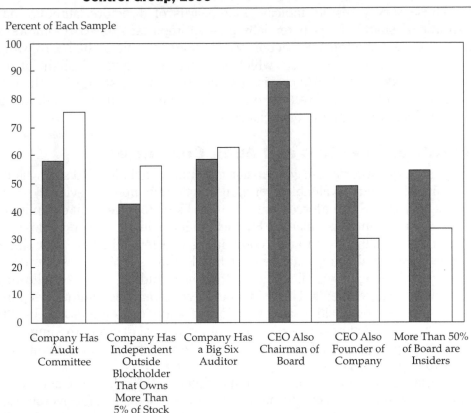

Percent of Each Sample

■ Enforcement Companies   □ Control Sample

Source: Dechow, Sloan, and Sweeney (1996).

had an insider-controlled board (i.e., more than 50 percent of the board members were insiders), and the chief executive officer (CEO) was more likely to be the chair of the board or the company founder. This characteristic suggests that the CEO was likely to have significant influence over the choice of board members.

Beasley (1996) confirmed the Dechow–Sloan–Sweeney (1996) finding that a higher percentage of outside directors is associated with a lower likelihood that the company will be subject to an enforcement action. He further found that outside directors are more effective at reducing the likelihood of GAAP violations when they have served on the board for a long period of time and when they have few other directorships.

These survey results indicate that boards of directors, auditors, and institutional shareholders potentially play an important role as monitors of earnings quality. In the next section, we examine the role of the board with a focus on the audit committee, which is especially relevant in light of the Sarbanes–Oxley Act of 2002 provisions that are meant to strengthen the role of the audit committee. We then discuss the roles of auditors, institutional investors, analysts, and the financial press.

Boards of Directors and Audit Committees

Early research on corporate governance generally concluded that strong audit committees provide a valuable oversight function. As noted previously, companies subject to SEC enforcement were less likely to have audit committees than nonenforcement companies. Further evidence in McMullen (1996) indicated that companies with audit committees had lower instances of shareholder litigation alleging management fraud, fewer earnings restatements, fewer SEC actions, fewer illegal acts, and lower auditor turnover following accounting disagreements. This evidence suggests that the minimum requirements for the composition and function of audit committees set by the Sarbanes–Oxley Act of 2002—presumably with a goal of strengthening audit committee quality, in particular, and corporate governance, in general—are likely to improve earnings quality.

Sarbanes–Oxley has four provisions related to the role of the audit committee. First, the act makes the audit committee responsible for oversight of the external audit function, including appointment and compensation of auditors and resolution of disagreements. Second, the audit committee members must be "independent"—not officers, employees, consultants, or advisors of the company or any of its affiliates. Third, one audit committee member must be a financial expert, as defined by the act. Fourth, the committee must have written procedures for dealing with internal audit questions; the purpose of this requirement is to promote (or at least not discourage) whistle-blowing.

Although it is too early to assess the direct impact of Sarbanes–Oxley on earnings quality, some earlier research is relevant to assessing the act's requirements in relation to earnings quality. For example, research supports the Sarbanes–Oxley provision that requires audit committee members to be independent. Klein (2002) found that companies with less independent audit committees—where an audit committee was defined as independent if the majority of its members were independent directors—have greater abnormal accruals, which she suggested is an indication of earnings management. In addition, she found that when companies reduce the independence of their audit committees, abnormal accruals increase, which strengthens the case that a direct association exists between audit committee independence and accruals.

Research evidence also supports the Sarbanes–Oxley requirement that companies must have a financial expert on the audit committee. Prior to Sarbanes–Oxley, the securities exchanges required that audit committees have at least one member with financial expertise and that the other committee members be financially literate. Sarbanes–Oxley requires that the SEC provide a definition of financial expertise and set minimum disclosures about the financial expertise of the audit committee members.[31] Myers (2001) showed that the existence of an audit committee per se does not improve earnings quality, when low-quality earnings are defined as those with large restructuring and other discretionary charges. She did find, however, that audit committees appear to be more effective in reducing the size of discretionary charges when the audit committee has at least one member who has accounting or related financial expertise or when the committee has outside directors who serve on few other boards.

In addition, McDaniel, Martin, and Maines (2002) showed in an experimental setting that financial experts (as defined by the stock exchanges prior to Sarbanes–Oxley) do, in fact, evaluate financial statements differently from the way those who are merely financially literate do. Financial literates are more likely to focus on issues that are currently being discussed in the financial press and on large and nonrecurring items, whereas financial experts focus not only on these items but also on less trendy issues and on recurring earnings. Thus, if the recent regulatory changes result in more real financial experts on audit committees, we expect an increase in earnings quality on average.

---

[31] The final rules defined an audit committee financial expert as a person who has the following attributes: (1) an understanding of GAAP and financial statements, (2) the ability to assess the general application of such principles in connection with the accounting for estimates, accruals, and reserves, (3) experience preparing, auditing, analyzing, or evaluating financial statements that present a breadth and level of complexity in accounting issues that are generally comparable to the breadth and complexity of issues that can reasonably be expected to be raised by the company's financial statements or experience actively supervising one or more persons engaged in such activities, (4) an understanding of internal controls and procedures for financial reporting, and (5) an understanding of audit committee functions. A person must have acquired such attributes through one or more of the following: (1) education and experience as a principal financial officer, principal accounting officer, controller, public accountant, or auditor or experience in one or more positions that involve the performance of similar functions, (2) experience actively supervising a principal financial officer, principal accounting officer, controller, public accountant, auditor, or person performing similar functions, (3) experience overseeing or assessing the performance of companies or public accountants with respect to the preparation, auditing, or evaluation of financial statements, or (4) other relevant experience.

In summary, evidence suggests that a strong audit committee (or, in the earlier studies, the *existence* of an audit committee) is associated with a lower incidence of fraud accusations in securities litigation, lower unusual accruals, and fewer SEC enforcement actions. These results suggest that weak audit committees provide managers with the opportunity to engage in earnings management.

Auditors

In an analysis of the relationship of the auditor to earnings quality, it is important to distinguish between the auditor's role and responsibility in the financial reporting process and the company's role and responsibility. The role of the auditor is to review the financial statements prepared by managers and determine (through various test procedures) whether they conform to GAAP. Management is responsible for preparation of the financial statements.

Managers are allowed to choose among accounting methods (e.g., straight-line versus accelerated depreciation) and among estimation techniques (e.g., using weekly or daily data to estimate stock return volatility to measure executive stock option expense). GAAP inherently includes flexibility, which is meant to improve the financial reporting system by making it not a "one size fits all" system. Managers can use their discretion to make the financial statements more relevant to users of the statements by making choices that enhance the ability of earnings to predict future cash flows. This flexibility means, however, that a company can report a range of earnings numbers, all of which are within the guidelines of GAAP. In other words, the flexibility of the system allows managers the opportunity to manipulate earnings without violating GAAP.

An auditor attests only to the fact that the financial statements "present fairly" the results of operations and the financial position of the company "in accordance with GAAP." An auditor does not state that the principles chosen, when there is a choice, provide the most relevant information. For any given company, a particular earnings component may not be useful for equity valuation because GAAP undermines its relevance. The accounting profession considers the readers of financial statements to be responsible for understanding GAAP well enough to detect when earnings lack relevance in any specific context. The auditor does, however, have the power to question assumptions (e.g., the size of allowances for returns) and forecasts (e.g., the useful life of equipment) made by management and to require changes before issuing a "clean" opinion. In this role, the auditor can significantly increase earnings quality, in addition to detecting violations of GAAP.

Overall Audit Quality. Before discussing the research on audit effectiveness, we offer one caveat about the conclusions that can be drawn: In general, researchers can execute only indirect tests of auditor effectiveness. They see only the outcome of an audit; they do not see what a company's financial statements would have looked like if they had not been audited or, in the extreme, if the managers had known the statements would not be audited. Some direct tests of auditor effectiveness can be made, but they must rely on surveys, proprietary datasets from audit companies, and experiments. Based on the existing research, it is impossible to know the extent to which auditors prevent earnings management. Any result on auditor effectiveness is likely to understate the contribution that auditors make to the overall level of financial reporting quality in the United States.

■ *Direct evidence.* Direct evidence of auditor effectiveness comes from (1) using proprietary datasets, (2) studying auditors in experimental settings, (3) conducting surveys, and (4) exploiting the rare situations in which audited data are available for some companies and unaudited but similar data are available for other companies. We cite one example of each of these types of research.

Kinney and Martin (1994) performed a meta-analysis of nine studies of auditor adjustments, all of which used proprietary datasets to identify adjusting entries that the auditors detected but may or may not have recorded. In total, the analysis encompassed 1,500 audits and 16 audit-years. Using 5 percent of net income or 0.5 percent of revenues or total assets as benchmarks for defining what was material, their analysis showed that average aggregate adjustments were two to eight times greater than the materiality threshold. In addition, audit adjustments were "overwhelmingly" negative; the average ratio of adjustments for earnings overstatements to adjustments for earnings understatements across the different studies was 1.41 to 1.61.

Hirst (1994) showed that 84 auditors from Big Six and other national audit firms, in an experimental setting, were sensitive to the earnings management incentives provided by management buyout opportunities and bonus plans. He also showed that auditors incorporate their understanding of earnings management incentives into their audit judgments.

Nelson, Elliott, and Tarpley (2003), in a study described in Chapter 5, questioned 253 auditors from one of the Big Five firms in 1998 and identified 515 experiences with clients in which the auditor suspected earnings management. Their results suggest that auditors are less likely to waive earnings management attempts that increase current-year income and more likely to waive the attempts that they view as immaterial or that are attempted by large clients. This study also found that managers are more likely to make earnings management attempts (and the auditor less likely to adjust attempts) that are structured to comply with "bright-line" GAAP rules or, at the other extreme, involve unstructured transactions and imprecise rules.[32] The authors found that managers are more likely to make income-decreasing adjustments when standards are imprecise; such standards offer managers an opportunity to create "reserves" that can be used in future years to boost earnings.

Finally, as to direct evidence, McConomy (1998) showed that managers' forecasts in Canadian prospectuses that are audited (as required by regulation in 1989) contain significantly less positive bias than forecasts that are simply subject to review. This study is one of the few that could, because of the circumstance, directly compare audited figures with reported but unaudited figures.

The conclusion from all four studies, which is generally supported by the extensive literature in this area, is that auditors have the ability to detect and prevent earnings management.

■ *Indirect evidence.* Although the direct evidence that auditors have the ability to be effective monitors is strong, the indirect evidence on whether these abilities translate into effective audits, specifically related to detecting earnings management, is mixed. Early studies showed a positive association between modified audit opinions and high abnormal accruals, and the studies interpreted this link as indirect evidence that auditors identified earnings management and communicated their detections to the public. More recent studies found no evidence, however, that auditors issue more qualified opinions for high-accrual companies, even though these companies tend to have more SEC enforcement actions taken against them (Bradshaw, Richardson, and Sloan 2001). Rather, the modified opinions associated with large abnormal accruals are "going concern" opinions related to financial distress; the "unusual" accruals are related to the distress and not necessarily an indication of earnings management (Butler, Leone, and Willenborg 2003).

Krishnan (2003) found an association between auditors with expertise in the company's industry and discretionary accruals. Auditors with industry expertise were associated with significantly lower "discretionary" accruals than auditors without the expertise. In addition, Myers, Myers, and Omer (2003) documented that auditors' tenure with the company being audited improves rather than weakens earnings quality. In their study, the companies with longer-tenure auditors had lower discretionary accruals after a multitude of potentially correlated variables were controlled for.

---

[32]Bright-line rules have precise "lines" that determine whether a company should apply one accounting treatment or another. Such rules allow transactions that are economically similar but vary slightly with respect to one feature (e.g., 74 percent or 76 percent of the leased asset's useful life) to be accounted for in very different ways. The exact point at which the line is drawn is arbitrary and does not necessarily capture the intent or complexities of different transactions.

The "Big" Firms vs. Other Auditors. Cross-sectional evidence indicates that audits by the Big accounting firms (the Big Eight, Six, or Five, depending on the sample period) are of higher quality than audits by other auditors (despite recent newsworthy cases).

In these studies, "quality" was measured in a variety of ways. One measure of quality was the magnitude of market reactions to earnings data or valuations of earnings; bigger reactions and higher valuations indicate that investors perceive the underlying earnings number to be of higher quality (Teoh and Wong 1993). Other measures of quality are more direct. Gaver and Paterson (2001) documented that insurers that used auditors and actuaries both of whom were from Big Six accounting firms essentially eliminated the problem of underreserves for losses. Becker, DeFond, Jiambalvo, and Subramanyam (1998) and Francis, Maydew, and Sparks (1999) documented that clients of non–Big Six auditors reported higher discretionary accruals (in absolute value) than clients of Big Six auditors. Palmrose (1988) studied 472 cases (183 resolutions) involving the 15 largest U.S. audit companies for 1960–1985. In this sample, the non–Big Eight companies, as a group, had a significantly higher litigation rate, based on allegations of audit failures, than the Big Eight companies. For the Big Eight companies, 3 percent of the estimated number of their public clients were involved in suits alleging audit failure; for the non–Big Eight companies, the rate was 5.1 percent. Even if only meritorious cases—those resolved through a payment by the audit companies—are considered, the difference between the two groups still showed a significantly lower litigation rate for the Big Eight companies: 1.9 percent versus 3.8 percent.

Auditor Changes. A change of auditors is generally viewed as a "red flag" about the quality of the financial statements because it suggests that management and the auditor have had some irreconcilable disagreement about the financial statements. DeFond and Subramanyam (1998) found evidence of significantly lower discretionary accruals in the year before a company changed auditors and more normal accruals in the new auditor's first year. One interpretation of this result is that companies fire their auditors when the auditor forces the company to be too conservative. Companies that change auditors are also frequently in financial distress, however, so determining their "normal" discretionary accruals is difficult. Either way, the DeFond–Subramanyam results suggest that an auditor change is potentially a red flag about earnings quality.

Not all auditor changes, however, are associated with a reported disagreement. DeFond and Jiambalvo (1993) compared companies that changed auditors and reported a disagreement with companies that changed auditors but reported no disagreement. They found that companies that changed auditors because of a reported disagreement are more likely to have debt covenant violations, have higher leverage, and have shown a decline in earnings. These companies have the greatest incentive to manage earnings and are more likely to use "disagreeable" accounting procedures. Thus, the authors interpreted the results as evidence that auditors detect attempts at earnings management and then resign (or are fired) if the disagreement over the earnings management cannot be resolved.

Impact of Nonaudit Services on Audit Quality. A topic of recent interest is whether audit quality is impaired when the auditor engages in nonaudit services for a client company. Some have alleged that the nonaudit fees make auditors beholden to their clients and compromise the auditors' independence. When auditors face a conflict of interest, it is likely that audit quality, and thus earnings quality, will suffer.

Clearly, documented cases of fraud and accounting scandal have been caused, or at least exacerbated, by problems with auditor independence. The empirical evidence in large samples, however, is mixed. Kinney, Palmrose, and Scholz (2003) examined a set of companies that issued accounting restatements and a control sample of companies that did not during the 1995–2000 period. For each company, they obtained confidential data from the seven largest U.S. auditing firms on fees for performing six services—audit, audit-related, internal audit, financial information system design and implementation (FISDI), tax, and other services. Their significant findings are that companies with an auditor that performs substantial tax advisory services are less likely to issue earnings restatements whereas restatements are positively correlated with "other" services. They suggested that tax advisory service creates less of a conflict of interest than consulting. They found no relationship between restatements and either internal audit fees or FISDI fees. These two services were restricted by the SEC as of November 2000. The authors concluded that the SEC's restrictions on internal audit and FISDI services were not necessary, but they acknowledged that significant "other" services potentially create a conflict. One final point that this study made is that approximately 95 percent of the registrants examined reported zero fees associated with FISDI and internal audit services. Only 27.8 percent of the registrants had nonzero "other" fees. The authors suggested that nonaudit fees are not a significant problem.

Frankel, Johnson, and Nelson (2002), however, suggested that nonaudit work by the auditing firm decreases earnings quality. They found a positive association between the magnitude of nonaudit fees and the likelihood that the audited companies met or beat analysts' forecasts. They also reported a positive association between nonaudit fees and the likelihood that a company would report large absolute discretionary accruals. These results are controversial, and a number of other papers have questioned the merits of this study on various dimensions. However, the results appear to stand up to scrutiny. For example, Ruddock, Sherwood, and Taylor (2004) used a sample of 1,963 company-year observations of Australian companies that reported audit fees since 1993. Their evidence suggests that companies with large discretionary accruals have an unusually high level of nonaudit fees.

Finally, there are studies of investor *perceptions* about nonaudit work done by the company's auditor. To summarize the literature in a few words, investors appear to see added value when the auditor does some—but only a small amount of—nonaudit work. One explanation for this result is that investors perceive spillover in knowledge to occur in such situations—as long as the work is not so extensive as to create a conflict of interest.

In summary, many researchers have investigated the role of the auditor in improving earnings quality. The results suggest that auditors are more likely to detect and adjust earnings management attempts when

- the GAAP rules contain few bright lines,
- the earnings management increases earnings,
- the auditor has experience within the industry and with the company,
- the auditor does not provide too many "other" services to the client, and
- the audit is done by one of the Big firms.

Institutional Investors

The evidence related to the role of institutional investors as monitors of earnings quality is limited, but a substantial body of literature has suggested that these investors are, on average, "more sophisticated" than individual investors. For example, Bartov, Radhakrishnan, and Krinsky (2000) showed that the cumulative abnormal return in the 60-day window following an earnings announcement is negatively correlated with the degree of institutional ownership. One interpretation of this result is that more information is impounded in price immediately at the time of the earnings announcement when investor sophistication (i.e., institutional ownership) is greatest. Another interpretation is that companies with a high proportion of institutional ownership announce higher-quality earnings, so fewer negative surprises afflict them in the postannouncement period. In general, using a variety of research designs, researchers have suggested that institutional investors understand earnings better than individual investors, but these studies do not specifically address whether institutional investors are better at detecting (or preventing) earnings management.

One paper that does provide compelling evidence that institutional investors serve a positive role in improving earnings quality is the study by Bushee (1998). He showed that companies that have low institutional ownership are more likely to cut research and development expenditures when earnings are abnormally low. Companies with greater institutional ownership do *not* cut R&D expenditures to offset bad earnings in a given period. He suggested that companies with low institutional ownership have an investor base that is, on average, less sophisticated and more myopically focused on total earnings than on the company's fundamental determinants. The presence of institutional owners decreases a company's incentives to play accounting "games."

An especially interesting result of this study is that the findings depend on the type of institutional investor. Institutional investors that engage in momentum trading strategies and have high portfolio turnover actually encourage R&D cuts when they hold large positions. Thus, these types of institutional investors should not be thought of as monitors of earnings quality. These results are especially important because the companies with low institutional ownership are not simply engaging in accounting gimmicks; they are sacrificing real economic programs in order to meet earnings objectives.

Analysts

Unlike auditors and audit committees, analysts do not play a formal role in supplying quality financial statements. As with institutional investors, however, their demand for high-quality data makes them an informal monitor of earnings quality.

Evidence of the effectiveness of analysts as monitors is difficult to find. A considerable body of literature shows systematic evidence of bias in analyst forecasts, which may indicate a lack of attention by analysts to earnings quality. **Figure 6.2** illustrates positive bias, on average, in analysts' earnings forecasts. Looking across all subperiods and regardless of the age of the forecast, the forecast errors are predominantly negative (i.e., an optimistic bias results when the forecast is subtracted from the actual). Figure 6.2 also illustrates, however, that analysts gradually revise their earnings forecasts down during the year, possibly so that companies can "beat" their forecasts. In the most recent period of this study, 1995–1998, the trend was actually to report pessimistic forecasts (i.e., positive forecast errors) as much as four months prior to the earnings announcement date. The authors of this study investigated possible motivations for managers to "walk down" consensus forecasts. Their evidence suggests that companies with the largest walk-downs are ones in which managers are selling their own insider holdings after the earnings announcement.

Figure 6.2. Median Earnings Forecast Error Scaled by Price, by Period

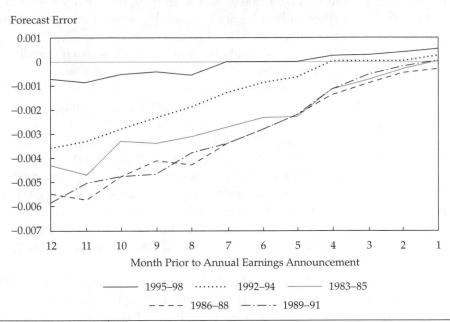

Notes: Forecast error is defined as actual earnings minus forecasted earnings. The sample consisted of all company-year observations with data available in the I/B/E/S detail files to construct a median consensus for the monthly periods leading up to the annual earnings announcement. All individual analyst forecasts were included except forecasts that created forecast errors greater than the stock price; that is, scaled forecasts greater than 100 percent were excluded from the consensus measure. Month 1 is the most recent month period prior to the annual earnings announcement.

Source: Richardson, Teoh, and Wysocki (2003).

Related specifically to detecting accruals management, Bradshaw, Richardson, and Sloan (2001) showed that sell-side analysts' earnings forecasts do not incorporate the average time-series information in accruals, even though companies with high accruals are more likely to experience earnings problems in future periods.

One explanation for the biases in forecasts, and for the fact that forecasts do not reflect the publicly available information in accruals, is that analysts consistently miss something, possibly because they do not have adequate information to forecast earnings or because they are naive. This interpretation of the evidence suggests that we should not expect analysts to be effective monitors of earnings quality. However, the biases have other explanations. Analyst incentives are not well understood. Analysts could be intentionally optimistic to encourage and promote underwriting business. Alternatively, analysts could be intentionally biased because of personal (compensation) incentives.[33] The biases indicate only that analysts are not now effective monitors. But perhaps they could be.

In fact, evidence of analysts' ability to detect earnings management in an experimental setting, where compensation incentives, for example, do not exist, indicates that analysts have expertise in detecting (and discounting) earnings management. Hirst and Hopkins (1998) showed that buy-side financial analysts discount valuations more for companies that appear to actively manage earnings related to available-for-sale securities. Their study focused on the benefits of separately reporting the components of comprehensive income. Thus, they made the point that analysts are better able to detect the earnings management attempts and incorporate this information into valuations when the gains and losses on available-for-sale security sales are separately reported. Nonetheless, their evidence suggests that analysts have the ability to detect earnings management of this type and to appropriately adjust valuations for it, which suggests that they have the ability to serve as effective monitors.

In summary, large-sample evidence suggests that analysts have biases similar to those of investors and are only slightly better than investors at identifying low-quality earnings. The fact that changes in analysts' stock recommendations and their earnings forecasts move stock prices suggests that the opinion of analysts matters to investors and that analysts could play a critical role in keeping managers honest and monitoring earnings quality.

The Press as Watchdog

In some cases, despite more formal monitoring by boards, auditors, institutional investors, and analysts, it is the financial press that first highlights an earnings-quality problem. And the press's role as watchdog should not be ignored.

Miller (2004) investigated types of accounting fraud that have been "caught" by the press. His sample consisted of companies identified by the SEC in Accounting and Auditing Enforcement Releases as having committed accounting fraud, misappropriated funds, or made materially misleading public statements. He considered a company to be caught by the press if an article that questioned the company's accounting appeared prior to public disclosure by the company (or the SEC) that an accounting problem existed. Approximately 30 percent of the fraud sample was caught by the press.

---

[33] Another explanation is that the optimism bias is simply a statistical phenomenon related to the available data and the measurement of forecast errors or an econometric issue related to self-selection of analyst coverage of certain types of companies. For an extensive discussion of this topic, see Abarbanell and Lehavy (2003).

Miller found that companies caught by the press have a richer information environment (i.e., more analysts follow these companies and more press articles are written about these companies). He argued that a rich information environment reduces the costs of an information search by the press. His evidence also suggests that the press is more likely to write an article about a company when the fraud is provocative (i.e., will sell newspapers), such as when managers misappropriate funds or make misleading public statements. Reporters do not generally uncover the fraud themselves; the press relies on many sources of information but particularly on analysts, lawsuits, and auditor changes. Miller's results suggest that the press plays a vital role as an information intermediary between formal monitors—analysts, auditors, and investors—and the general public.

7. Investor Response to Earnings

In this chapter, we present research evidence on how investors respond to earnings data. If investors are rational in their response to earnings, then we would not expect markets to respond to low-quality earnings. Therefore, the process of predicting and understanding how investors respond to earnings has implications for understanding earnings quality.

We first provide evidence on the statistical time-series properties of earnings, which provides a benchmark for what investors should understand about the persistence of earnings, on average, for large samples of companies. Evidence on a post-earnings-announcement drift in returns suggests that investors do not fully incorporate information about the time-series properties of quarterly earnings into prices when the earnings are announced—especially for small companies and for companies with extreme earnings changes. We next discuss research examining the causes of cross-sectional variation in stock price reactions to earnings news. The results provide an understanding of how company characteristics or characteristics of the news affect market reactions and, therefore, help equip an analyst to predict reactions to earnings surprises.

Post-Earnings-Announcement Drift

A long history of research on quarterly earnings indicates that earnings have a seasonal component and an adjacent quarter-to-quarter component (e.g., Foster 1977; Griffin 1977; Brown and Rozeff 1979). Bernard and Thomas (1990) provided a nice numerical summary of the relationships: Define $\Delta Q_{t,t-4}$ as the earnings for quarter t minus the earnings for quarter $t-4$ (i.e., the year-over-year change in quarterly earnings). Bernard and Thomas documented the following company-specific autocorrelations:

	Correlation of $\Delta Q_{t,t-4}$ with		
$\Delta Q_{t-1,t-5}$ (one lag)	$\Delta Q_{t-2,t-6}$ (two lags)	$\Delta Q_{t-3,t-7}$ (three lags)	$\Delta Q_{t-4,t-8}$ (four lags)
0.34	0.19	0.06	−0.24

They also provided a simple example to aid in the interpretation of these autocorrelations. Assume a company had the following actual earnings per share (EPS) in 1998:

	Q1	Q2	Q3	Q4
EPS	10.00	10.00	10.00	20.00

The company then announced earnings of $11.00 for Q1 of 1999. Thus, $\Delta Q_{t,t-4}$ would be $1.00. Assuming no linear growth trend, the implications for forecasts for 1999 and 2000 are as follows:

	Q1	Q2	Q3	Q4
1999 EPS	11.00 (actual)	10.34	10.19	20.06
2000 EPS	10.76			

Of the $1.00 change in earnings from Q1 of 1998, $0.34 would be expected to persist for one future quarter, $0.19 to persist into the second future quarter, and $0.06 to persist into the third future quarter. The forecast for the fourth future quarter would be a reversal of $0.24. If current EPS are $11.00, the year-ahead Q1 forecast would be

$11.00 – $0.24 = $10.76.

Following Brown and Rozeff, Bernard and Thomas produced the following expectations model for next quarter's earnings:

$$E(Q_t) = \delta + Q_{t-4} + \phi(Q_{t-1} - Q_{t-5}) + \vartheta \epsilon_{t-4}. \tag{7.1}$$

In other words, earnings at quarter t are expected to be equal to a trend component, δ, because companies tend to grow through time, plus a proportion, ϕ, of the change in last quarter's year-over-year earnings that captures the positive serial correlation for the first three lags of earnings, plus a moving average term, ϑ, that captures the reversal in the fourth lag.

Bernard and Thomas examined stock return reactions to earnings announcements to determine whether investors use this model or a simpler model to predict earnings. The simpler model is a seasonal random walk model (i.e., earnings this quarter are expected to be the same as earnings in the same quarter from the prior year plus some trend component):

$$E(Q_t) = \delta + Q_{t-4}. \tag{7.2}$$

In the example, the forecasts for 1999 and 2000 from the seasonal random walk model are

	Q1	Q2	Q3	Q4
1999 EPS	11.00 (actual)	10.00	10.00	20.00
2000 EPS	11.00			

The predictable earnings surprises are

	Q1	Q2	Q3	Q4
1999 EPS	1.00 (known)	0.34	0.19	0.06
2000 EPS	–0.24			

Bernard and Thomas found evidence of market reactions at earnings announcement dates that are correlated with these predictable earnings surprises. This result was stronger for small companies, which are likely to have fewer analysts following them. That is, investors are surprised by the earnings that are announced and their surprise is reflected in the stock price. But these earnings would not be unexpected if investors had used the more accurate time-series model (Equation 7.1) rather than the seasonal random walk model (Equation 7.2). Thus, Bernard and Thomas's evidence suggests that investors use the naive random walk model to predict earnings.

Bernard and Thomas ranked companies into deciles based on their quarterly earnings surprises. A strategy of purchasing companies in the top 10 percent of positive earnings surprises and selling companies in the bottom 10 percent of negative earnings surprises yielded a hedge return of 8.6 percent. More than 21 percent of this return occurred in the three-day periods surrounding the next three earnings announcements. Bernard and Thomas suggested that naive earnings expectations are likely to be important for explaining post-earnings-announcement drift.[34]

Additional studies have examined whether analysts understand the time-series properties of earnings. Brown, Hagerman, Griffin, and Zmijewski (1987b) provided early evidence that analysts' forecasts of quarterly earnings outperform univariate time-series models. They suggested that the superiority of the analysts stems from their ability to update their forecasts of quarterly earnings as nonearnings information becomes available.

In contrast, Abarbanell and Bernard (1992) suggested that analysts do not incorporate the predictable seasonal component of earnings into their forecasts. They examined Value Line forecast errors for 178 companies for up to 44 quarters in the 1976–86 period. The forecast errors were positively autocorrelated over the first three lags with declining magnitude. This autocorrelation pattern is consistent with an underreaction to earnings that follow a seasonal random walk. The magnitude of the autocorrelation in analysts' forecast errors was not large enough, however, to explain post-earnings-announcement drift.

Fourth-quarter earnings are significantly different from earnings for the first three quarters for (at least) two reasons. First, the fourth quarter is more likely than other quarters to contain special items, such as asset impairment charges or restructuring charges. **Figure 7.1** illustrates that special items as a proportion of total expenses are higher in the fourth quarter. **Figure 7.2**

---

[34]The post-earnings-announcement drift was observable in data as early as the study by Ball and Brown (1968) and was well known prior to Bernard and Thomas's work. For example, see Joy, Litzenberger, and McEnally (1977).

Figure 7.1. Proportion of Special Items Relative to Total Expenses, 1985–97

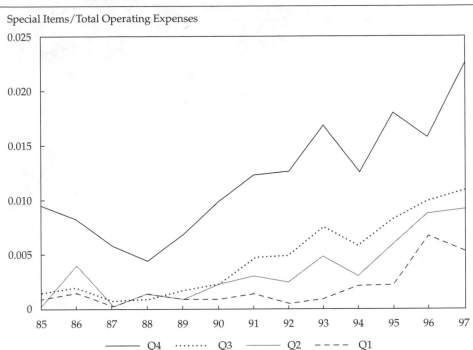

Special Items/Total Operating Expenses

Notes: Cross-sectional means. Sample size was 98,647 company-quarter observations. Special items (data item #32) and total operating expenses, defined as the difference between sales (data item #2) and pretax income (data item #23), are from Compustat quarterly research tapes.

Source: Bradshaw and Sloan (2002).

indicates that a greater proportion of companies report losses in the fourth quarter than in other quarters. These figures suggest that fourth-quarter earnings are likely to be less persistent than, to be of lower quality than, and to behave differently from earnings of other quarters.

Second, the fourth quarter is different because the time-series properties of quarterly earnings are affected by the use of the *integral method* of accounting. U.S. generally accepted accounting principles (GAAP) require that each quarterly reporting period be viewed as an integral part of the annual reporting period. The integral method smooths across quarters what would otherwise be lumpy revenues or expenses. Companies must estimate many annual operating expenses and allocate these estimates to interim periods on the basis of forecasted annual figures, such as sales. Expenses that are commonly estimated include cost of goods sold, income tax expense, and amortization.

Figure 7.2.   Frequency of Quarterly Losses, 1978–2001

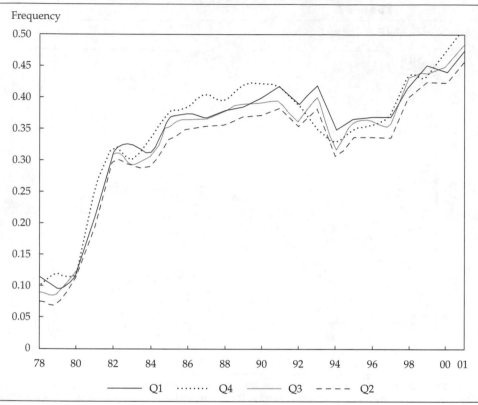

Source: Data from Compustat.

A consequence of the integral approach is that errors in earnings estimates are likely to be correlated across the first three quarters and then reversed or corrected in the fourth quarter. An implication of the integral approach is that the serial correlation in quarterly earnings is likely to be stronger for quarters within the same fiscal year. If Company A announces a positive year-over-year earnings change in Q1, the analyst should expect positive and declining year-over-year earnings changes for Q2, Q3, and Q4 and a negative earnings change for Q1 of the following year. If Company B announces a positive earnings change in Q4, the analyst should recognize that the implication for one-quarter-ahead earnings (Q1 earnings in the subsequent year) is weaker than if the positive change were for Q1–Q3.

Rangan and Sloan (1998) verified this intuition. They showed that the serial correlation in quarterly earnings is approximately 50 percent larger when the lagged quarters are in the same fiscal year. And investor underreactions to predictable patterns in quarterly earnings are actually stronger than those documented by Bernard and Thomas when the "predictable" pattern takes into account whether the quarters are in the same fiscal year. **Figure 7.3** shows cumulative abnormal returns (CARs) to earnings announcements across all quarters in Rangan and Sloan's sample, pooled and then separately, for Q1 observations and Q4 observations. The sample consists of 172,564 firm-quarter observations in the years 1971–1994. The CARs are for a hedge portfolio that took a long position in the highest decile of seasonally differenced quarterly earnings deflated by the market value of equity (that is, "standardized unexpected earnings" or SUE) stocks and a corresponding short position in the lowest-decile SUE stocks. The top plot in Figure 7.3 is the CAR following the first fiscal quarter earnings announcements, the middle plot is the CAR following all earnings announcements, and the bottom plot is the CAR following fourth fiscal quarter earnings announcements. Each plot is divided into eight segments. The first segment measures the return from the second day following the earnings announcement date to the day three days before the following quarter's earnings announcement date. The second

Figure 7.3.   Four-Quarter Cumulative Abnormal Returns Following Different Fiscal Quarters' Earnings Announcements, 1971–94

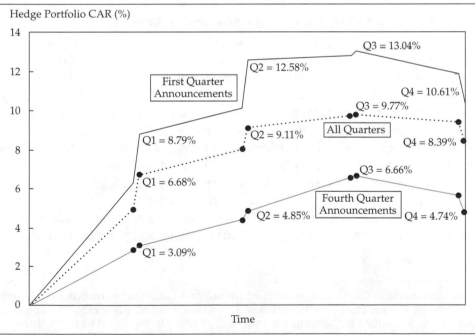

Note: Data for 172,564 company-quarter observations in the period.

Source: Rangan and Sloan (1998).

segment measures the three-day announcement period for the following quarter's earnings. The remaining six segments do the same for the following three quarters. The end point of the second segment is referred to as Q1 and equals the cumulative return through the following quarter's earnings announcement. Similarly, Q2, Q3, and Q4 refer to the CAR through the announcement of earnings for the second, third, and fourth quarters following the original earnings announcement.

Figure 7.3 shows that the predictable reaction to earnings surprises is much stronger in the first quarter than in the fourth quarter, which suggests that investors do not recognize the stronger time-series correlation of earnings for quarters within the same fiscal year.[35]

In summary, forecasts of quarterly earnings will be more accurate if they consider the serial correlation in earnings across quarters. The fourth quarter is very different from the first three quarters and includes a much greater proportion of transitory components. Investors are not completely aware of the time-series properties of quarterly earnings. Results of research indicate that post-earnings-announcement drift is stronger in small companies, in companies followed by few analysts, and in companies supported by few institutional investors.

Market Reactions to Unexpected Earnings

Researchers have been examining the relationship between stock returns and earnings at least since the publication of Ball and Brown (1968). The approaches have varied, with the more recent work focusing on earnings response coefficients. An earnings response coefficient is a measure of how investors respond to earnings news. When earnings are more value relevant, one would expect a stronger investor response. Thus, earnings response coefficients can be viewed as a measure of earnings quality. Investor reactions to earnings are affected by other factors however, not solely the value relevance of earnings. We discuss this concern in more detail later.

Setting this concern aside for now, we consider the evidence on cross-sectional differences in earnings response coefficients, which indicate how investors perceive various components of earnings and perceive earnings for

---

[35]Narayanamoorthy (2003) provided further insight into the time-series properties of quarterly earnings. He showed that the serial correlation in quarterly earnings is smaller for companies announcing a loss than for companies announcing positive earnings. And he found the effect to be incremental to the results documented by Rangan and Sloan. Thus, future serial correlation in quarterly earnings is stronger for earnings reported in the same fiscal year and for companies reporting positive earnings.

different types of companies. Researchers implement the following model to estimate investor response to earnings:

Stock return$_t$ = α + δ(Earnings surprise$_t$) + ϵ_t,   (7.3)

where δ is the earnings response coefficient (ERC). The stock return is measured either over a few days around the earnings announcement or over the same period as the earnings. The ERC measures how investors react to earnings surprises. A larger ERC indicates that a dollar of earnings surprise has greater valuation implications.

The earnings surprise (usually scaled by the market value of equity) is measured in a number of ways. The most common measures are the deviation of actual earnings from a predicted amount based on a time-series model of earnings and the deviation of actual earnings from the consensus analyst forecast (analyst forecast error). Several studies (e.g., Brown, Hagerman, Griffin, and Zmijewski 1987a) have provided evidence of the ability of various expectations models to explain stock returns.

ERCs as Proxies for the Quality of Earnings. Imhoff (1992) suggested that a strong earnings response coefficient is an indication of higher-quality earnings. To measure earnings quality, Imhoff used judgments obtained from security analysts who were members of the Financial Analysts Federation in 1983. The analysts were specialists in particular industries and were asked to rank companies in each industry on the basis of each company's accounting quality. Imhoff found that companies that had higher rankings had larger ERCs.

The results of DeFond and Park (2001) are also consistent with the interpretation of the ERC as a measure of earnings quality. They argued that if the market anticipates the reversing nature of abnormal working capital accruals, then ERCs will depend on whether abnormal accruals are positive (income increasing) or negative (income decreasing). They found higher ERCs when abnormal accruals suppressed the magnitude of earnings surprises and lower ERCs when abnormal accruals exaggerated the magnitude of earnings surprises. Thus, they concluded that investors deem high accruals to be an indication of low earnings quality and lower their response to earnings accordingly.

The results of Lev and Thiagarajan (1993) also suggest that ERCs are associated with earnings quality. They investigated the association between ERCs and fundamental signals that analysts often use. These signals include growth in inventory, accounts receivable, or selling, general, and administrative expenses (SG&A) greater than sales growth; growth in capital expenditures greater than the industry average; and whether the company uses LIFO (last in, first out) accounting for inventory. They found ERCs to be greater for companies where fundamental signals have positive implications for future earnings.

A high ERC does not necessarily, however, imply high earnings quality. The ERC is a measure of how earnings are capitalized into stock price, so it reflects characteristics not only of the earnings but also of the capitalization (or discount) rate (Collins and Kothari 1989). A mechanical issue associated with interpreting an ERC as a measure of earnings quality is that the "earnings surprise" is measured with error in the regression used to estimate the ERC (Equation 7.3). For example, measurement error in the earnings surprise coefficient from time-series models is lower, on average, for small companies than for large companies (Easton and Zmijewski 1989; Collins and Kothari). For small companies, less additional information is gathered and (presumably) impounded into price between earnings announcements, so a time-series model of earnings expectations fits the data better than it does for large companies, where earnings are only one piece of information being considered by the market. Thus, regressions that measure earnings surprises by using time-series models will show greater reactions to earnings announcements for small companies, even though their earnings may not differ in quality from those of large companies. Characteristics other than company size are also correlated with measurement error in the earnings surprise but are not necessarily indications of higher or lower earnings quality.[36]

Despite these caveats, the study of earnings response coefficients is a prolific area of accounting research. The basic premise is that more persistent (and value-relevant) earnings will have greater ERCs, so the purpose of many studies is to identify characteristics associated with persistence. In the next section, we discuss some of the key results on ERCs that provide insights into earnings persistence.

ERCs as Proxies for Earnings Persistence. A basic finding in the literature is that earnings that exhibit greater persistence have greater earnings multipliers (i.e., stock price multiples). Therefore, models that allow for differences in earnings multipliers based on persistence yield a higher statistical association between earnings and observed equity values than models that do not. The studies that led to these findings defined the persistence of a given income statement component by using either statistical models (Kormendi and Lipe 1987; O'Hanlon, Poon, and Yaansah 1992; Ramesh and Thia-

---

[36]For example, Skinner (1990) found that companies that have option initiations have lower ERCs because a great deal of information is gathered about the companies prior to the earnings release. Mendenhall and Fehrs (1999) found the opposite result for more recent data.

garajan 1993) or intuition (Lipe 1986; Bublitz and Ettredge 1989; Wild 1992). For example, Lipe decomposed earnings into gross profit, SG&A, interest expense, taxes, and other items and evaluated the persistence of each component. He showed that the market reaction to each component depends on the component's persistence.

Freeman and Tse (1992) documented that the marginal stock price response to unexpected earnings declines as the magnitude of the earnings surprise, in absolute value, increases. They also documented that the explanatory power of a model that allows for this nonlinear relationship is higher than that of a linear model of earnings surprises and stock prices. In other words, beating or missing expectations by a small amount will generate a bigger stock price response per dollar than beating or missing by a lot. Their explanation for this result was that larger earnings surprises in either direction are more likely to represent transitory or less persistent earnings than small surprises. Given this assumption, their results can be interpreted as evidence that stock prices reflect lower multipliers on less persistent earnings (see also Subramanyam 1996b; Lipe, Bryant, and Widener 1998).

Biddle and Seow (1991), following work done by Lev (1983), showed that ERCs are higher in industries that have high growth potential, have high barriers to entry, and produce nondurable goods. They argued that these variables are correlated with greater earnings persistence. They also showed that ERCs are lower in industries with high financial and operating leverage (i.e., industries with high costs of capital).

An interesting strand of the ERC literature proposes that earnings persistence can be viewed as a choice that a company makes. In particular, the studies predicted that losses are less persistent than profits because companies are more likely to abandon (or restructure) operations that generate losses. Hayn (1995) was one of the first to examine the effect of this "abandonment option" on ERCs. She hypothesized that, as a result of the abandonment option, investors would react more strongly to unexpected profits than to unexpected losses. Her results strongly supported this hypothesis.

Related evidence suggests that stock price responses to earnings surprises are negatively related to Altman's Z-score, a measure of bankruptcy probability. Subramanyam and Wild (1996) predicted this negative relationship on the basis of an argument that the earnings surprise is expected to persist over fewer periods (has a shorter "revision horizon") for the companies that are less likely to continue as going concerns.

Following Hayn, many researchers investigated whether book value of equity on the balance sheet is more important than earnings on the income statement for valuation of companies reporting losses (e.g., Collins, Maydew, and Weiss 1997; Subramanyam and Venkatachalam 1998; Burgstahler and Dichev 1997a; Collins, Pincus, and Xie 1999). These studies argued that the earnings of the "loss companies" are of relatively low quality in terms of predictive ability because those companies are likely to abandon operations that are incurring losses. Thus, current-period earnings are not representative of future performance and discounted earnings and cash flow models are not useful for predicting firm value. Current-period book value may be more relevant. The results supported this contention.

A second subset of research related to loss companies also predicts that these companies will have lower earnings persistence than "profit companies" but not because of an abandonment option. Basu (1997) suggested that "conservative" accounting—in Basu's definition, accounting that recognizes bad news in earnings more quickly than good news—leads to lower persistence of negative earnings changes. The intuition behind his argument is that revenues, gains, and anticipated gains are frequently recorded over multiple periods as they are "earned." Thus, positive earnings news in one period is likely to imply positive earnings news in the next when further recognition of earnings is allowed. Costs and anticipated losses, however, generally must be recognized in full as soon as they are identified. Because all (or most) of the loss is recorded in the current period, it has no implications for earnings in future periods.

ERCs and Company Characteristics. A significant company characteristic associated with ERCs—not surprisingly—is growth. A dollar of earnings surprise has greater implications for future earnings in high-growth companies than in low-growth companies (Collins and Kothari). Although this general finding does not reveal much about earnings quality, further analysis of this result by Skinner and Sloan (2002) does. They showed that the market reacts more strongly to earnings announcements of a given size for companies with high market values to book values and that the reaction to "bad news" earnings surprises for these growth companies is especially strong (and negative). The study did not address whether the cause is unrealistic forecasts of growth prior to the earnings announcement or whether the market over- or underreacts to the earnings surprise.

ERCs also vary with the source of unexpected earnings. Ertimur, Livnat, and Martikainen (2003) showed that stock prices react more strongly to earnings surprises driven by unexpected revenue increases than surprises driven by unexpected expense decreases. This result was particularly strong for growth companies. Their interpretation of the result was that investors view revenue increases to be of higher quality than expense decreases.

ERCs are also associated with company characteristics that are potential indicators of financial distress. Choi and Jeter (1992) showed that the ERC is lower for a company that receives a qualified audit opinion. This result has two possible explanations. One possibility is that it is more difficult to know the implications of current earnings for future earnings in a "qualified company." A second possibility is that companies that receive a qualified audit opinion have less-persistent earnings (are likely to be reporting losses), so the earnings surprise has less implication for the future.

Core and Schrand (1999), using option-pricing theory, argued that the greatest impact of earnings news should occur when companies are near default, just as the delta of an option (the change in the value of the option for a given change in stock price) is greatest at the option's strike price. The intuition behind this claim is that earnings can provide two pieces of value-relevant information: news about future cash flows and news about the company's probability of default. The impact of the second news is most important around the point of default. In other words, a negative earnings surprise is bad news, but it is even worse news when the company is close to defaulting on an earnings-based debt covenant. Similarly, a positive earnings surprise is especially good news when the company is near meeting an earnings-based debt covenant. Core and Schrand found that ERCs were larger in magnitude for savings and loan institutions that were close to violating capital requirements than for those that were not.

In summary, the responsiveness of stock prices to earnings announcements is a function of the market's assessment of the persistence of earnings. Persistence is a function of the underlying economics of the business, but it also depends on the reliability and quality of the management that produced the financial statements.

8. The Role of Voluntary Disclosure

Companies can use voluntary disclosure as a complement to the information required in financial statements to improve investor confidence and enhance an analyst's ability to forecast earnings. Voluntary disclosures are those for which managers have discretion over the nature, content, or timing. Voluntary disclosures include conference calls, preannouncements of earnings, press releases, *pro forma* earnings, and management forecasts of earnings. Although most large companies use webcasts or conference calls to discuss quarterly financial information, the extent to which these vehicles are actually "informative" is a matter of managerial discretion. Voluntary disclosures also include reports of information within the financial statements that exceed what is strictly required under generally accepted accounting principles (GAAP). When earnings are of low quality and do not do a good job of reflecting a company's operating performance, voluntary disclosures can be especially useful to market participants.

The U.S. Securities and Exchange Commission requires companies with registered securities to make certain disclosures. Companies commit to periodic filings of their financial performance on Form 10-K (annual financials) and Form 10-Q (quarterly financials) in accordance with GAAP. Companies have a duty to update or correct preexisting disclosures (such as those made on a Form 8-K) under Rule 10b-5 of the Securities Exchange Act of 1934. The exchanges also impose disclosure requirements. The New York Stock Exchange, for example, requires timely disclosure of material information, in general, and sets forth rules on the method and timing of information releases. In addition to these mandatory disclosures, companies have many opportunities to make voluntary disclosures that can enhance earnings quality.

An important point about voluntary disclosure is that more disclosure does not always make analysts and investors better off. More public disclosure by a company can reduce incentives for individuals to gather private information, because the expected benefits from trading on the private information are reduced. Thus, public dissemination of information may level the playing field for all investors, but it may decrease the total amount of information that is available about a company and, presumably, reflected in its stock price. Another prominent argument proposes that variation among investors in terms of their ability to analyze financial information implies that additional disclosures lead to more variation in how these investors interpret a company's performance. Hence, more disclosure results in greater information asymmetry among investors at the time of an announcement. The sophisticated investors (who can interpret the information more accurately) are able to take advantage of uninformed investors. (See Kim and Verrecchia 1994 for a theoretical discussion of this point and Lee, Mucklow, and Ready 1993 for empirical evidence.) Finally, Bushee and Noe (2000) found that increasing disclosure can attract transient institutional investors to the company's stock and increase stock price volatility.

The literature on the determinants and consequences of voluntary disclosure is immense.[37] We focus on three issues associated with voluntary disclosure that are directly related to earnings quality as it affects an analyst's ability to forecast earnings:

1. Do managers' forecasts of earnings improve forecast accuracy?
2. Do other forms of management "guidance" improve forecast accuracy?
3. How has Regulation Fair Disclosure (Reg FD) affected managers' disclosure policies and the ability of analysts to forecast earnings?

Managers' Forecasts and Forecast Accuracy

Managers frequently provide voluntary disclosures related to their mandatory earnings announcements. These disclosures can be provided prior to an earnings announcement, presumably to adjust expectations and avoid disappointments. They can also be provided concurrent with earnings announcements to help analysts and investors interpret the announced numbers. We refer to such announcements as management "guidance" about earnings. The primary objective of management guidance—including management earnings forecasts in press releases or through private communications to analysts prior to Reg FD—is to improve the accuracy of earnings forecasts.

The literature on management forecasts is extensive, but we summarize research on three key findings: (1) management forecasts are informative; (2) management forecasts are "strategic"; and (3) management forecasts are biased.[38]

Management Forecasts Are Informative. Direct evidence indicates that management forecasts improve analyst forecast accuracy (e.g., Waymire

---

[37] See Verrecchia (2001) and Healy and Palepu (2001) for reviews of the literature.

[38] *Pro forma* earnings, a specific form of management guidance intended to guide readers to consider certain components of earnings to be more relevant than others, are discussed in Chapter 9.

1986). Williams (1996) showed that the extent of analysts' revisions is a function of managers' prior forecast accuracy. She suggested that managers establish a forecasting reputation based on prior earnings forecasts.

Management forecasts can also be inferred to be informative on the basis of evidence that they cause stock price reactions (e.g., Penman 1980; Pownall and Waymire 1989). Hoskin, Hughes, and Ricks (1986) investigated press releases made concurrently with earnings announcements. Their study showed that the stock market reacts to the news in announcements made concurrently with the announcement of annual earnings, which supports the argument that these disclosures provide relevant interpretive information. They found that announcements about earnings components have a significant impact on returns, which suggests that through disclosure, managers do (or at least investors perceive that they do) improve earnings quality. Announcements of dividend increases, prospective comments by key company officers, and prospective operating data also have a significant impact on stock price, which suggests that managers can enhance earnings quality through credible signals about the future.[39]

Hutton, Miller, and Skinner (2003) also provided evidence of the importance of supplementary disclosures in forecasts. They defined two categories of supplemental disclosures—verifiable forward-looking disclosures and "soft talk" disclosures, which cannot be verified *ex post*. They found that companies are more likely to supplement good news with a verifiable forward-looking disclosure and that the market responds to the good news forecasts only when they are accompanied by such statements. Together, these findings suggest that investors do not unconditionally perceive good news forecasts as credible; thus, managers have incentives to make them credible through additional disclosure.

Management Forecasts Are Strategic. Managers can be strategically self-serving with respect to forecasts along three important dimensions: existence, timing, and content. That is, do they choose to forecast at all, and if so, when and what? Research evidence (to be summarized) suggests that managers are "strategic" in their forecasting decisions and that their strategy is related to whether the news in the forecast is good or bad. The findings we discuss address a wide range of possible strategic behaviors.

Skinner (1994) showed that companies manage the content of their forecasts as a function of whether they are reporting positive or negative news. He investigated 93 NASDAQ companies in 1981–1990. Good news disclosures

---

[39]Prior research also has documented that interim forecasts are more informative than annual forecasts (Pownall, Wasley, and Waymire 1993).

tended to be point or range estimates of annual earnings per share (EPS), whereas bad news disclosures tended to be qualitative statements about the current quarter's earnings. The bad news forecasts had a larger effect on stock prices than the good news forecasts. The announcements of large negative earnings were preempted by a prior warning about 25 percent of the time, whereas other earnings announcements were preempted less than 10 percent of the time. Skinner argued that managers are more likely to disclose bad news because the news bears reputational costs as well as potential litigation costs.

Kasznik and Lev (1995) also suggested that strategic behavior is a function of the sign of the news and related this strategic behavior to fear of litigation. They focused on strategic behavior with respect to making or not making a disclosure (i.e., existence), rather than on the content of disclosures.[40] They selected companies with large earnings surprises and investigated whether the managers had provided warnings to investors of the impending surprises. They found that fewer than 10 percent of the large-surprise companies published quantitative earnings or sales forecasts and 50 percent remained silent. Companies facing earnings disappointments were more likely to make a disclosure, and larger disappointments were preceded by managerial forecasts that were more quantitative in nature. Warnings were more likely in the high-technology industry, for large companies, for companies where the earnings disappointment was more permanent in nature, and for companies where managers had made a previous forecast.

Soffer, Thiagarajan, and Walther (2000) also documented strategic patterns in forecasting associated with the sign of the news; their focus was on the strategic timing of the disclosure. They found that managers who disclose bad news tend to release essentially all of their news at the preannouncement date whereas managers with good news release only about half of the good news at that time. The authors suggested that by timing the bad news and good news disclosures in this way, companies suffer an overall smaller negative stock price reaction to bad news than if they waited to release the bad news at the earnings announcement date.[41]

Two additional papers focused on the strategic timing of forecasts around particular events. Frankel, McNichols, and Wilson (1995) predicted that companies that frequently raise external financing would strategically provide

---

[40]Miller (2002) suggested with respect to voluntary disclosures in general that "existence" of a disclosure is strategic and a function of the nature of the news. He found that companies are more likely to make voluntary disclosures—not limited to earnings forecasts—when times are good, which he defined as eight contiguous quarters of seasonally adjusted earnings increases.
[41]This result contrasts with the finding of Kasznik and Lev, who suggested that investors may overreact to managerial warnings of bad news. They posited that concerns over an overreaction may explain why about half of their sample did not provide any information before the bad news surprise.

more management forecasts. The forecasts, presumably, reduce information asymmetry problems and thus lower the company's cost of capital, an effect that provides the greatest benefit to companies that frequently raise external financing. They documented a positive association between management forecasts and subsequent issues of external financing over long horizons. They also found that management forecasts are not overly optimistic and that managers do not issue forecasts close to the time of an offering. They suggested that reputation and litigation concerns mitigate incentives to be overly optimistic.

Aboody and Kasznik (2000) investigated whether managers time forecasts on the basis of the timing of stock option awards. They focused on a sample of 2,039 option awards to chief executive officers by 572 companies with fixed award schedules. Managers cannot time the awards, but they do have discretion over the timing of information releases around the fixed award dates. Managers have incentives to reduce the company's stock price temporarily at the award date to establish an artificially low strike price for an at-the-money award. This insight led the authors to predict that managers will release bad news before the award date and good news after the award date. They found that stock returns and revisions in analysts' forecasts are consistent with this prediction. They also found the same pattern in a small sample of management forecasts. This evidence suggests that managers can act in their own self-interest in the timing of information releases.

Management Forecasts Are Biased. On average, management forecasts are pessimistic, when "pessimistic" means that actual earnings turn out to be higher than forecasted earnings, but the average hides some important time-series and cross-sectional patterns in forecasts. **Figure 8.1** illustrates various trends in forecasting behavior by time period. Management forecasts are becoming more pessimistic. As Figure 8.1 shows, Cotter, Tuna, and Wysocki (2003) documented an optimistic forecast bias in the 1993–97 period but a pessimistic bias in the sample periods after that. The pessimistic bias was stronger after Reg FD than before it. The authors separately reported that managers were pessimistic whether they were reporting good news or bad.

Cotter et al. found that analysts, on average, do not appear to adjust for this bias. They make earnings forecasts that are, on average, equal to the management forecast, and this trend has become even more pronounced since Reg FD. Tan, Libby, and Hunton (2002) also documented that analysts do not adjust their forecasts for the pessimistic bias in management forecasts.

Cotter et al. suggested that managers have an incentive to make pessimistic forecasts: They can later report small positive earnings surprises. As we discussed in Chapter 5, companies perceive meeting or beating targets to be

Figure 8.1. Proportion of Pessimistic, On-Target, and Optimistic Management EPS Forecasts, Various Periods

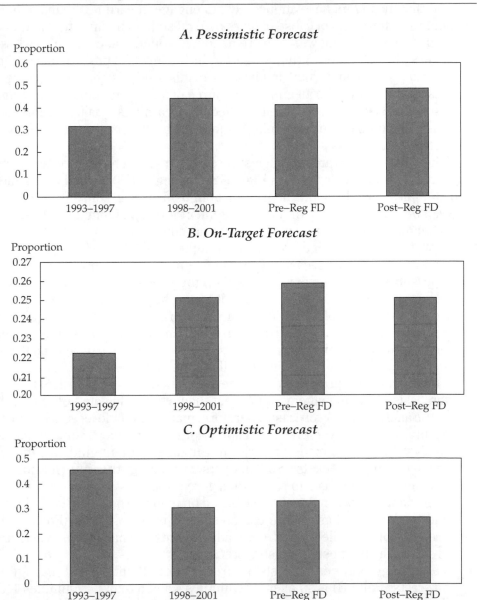

Notes: Sample was 2,876 management forecasts of quarterly EPS. Pre–Reg FD period is November 1998 through December 1999 (14 months); post–Reg FD period is November 2000 through December 2001 (14 months).

Source: Cotter, Tuna, and Wysocki (2003).

beneficial, and guiding forecasts down is one way to accomplish this goal. The other way to meet or beat a forecast is to manage earnings. Kasznik (1999) argued that managers have an incentive to engage in earnings management to meet their forecasts because of fears of legal actions by investors and loss of reputation. Consistent with this prediction, he found that companies whose managers overestimated earnings had significant levels of positive discretionary accruals.[42] An important implication of his study is that management forecasts, which could be an important source of information to investors and analysts, can also have detrimental effects on earnings quality. A forecast "commits" a company to an earnings number, so it increases the incentives for managing earnings.

The relationships among analyst forecasts, management forecasts, and forecast revisions are depicted in **Figure 8.2**. Feng (2003) ranked companies into quintiles based on the degree of optimism in the consensus analyst forecast before the release of the management forecast. Quintile 1 consisted of the companies with the most optimistic consensus forecasts (i.e., the forecasts that, if unchanged, would have resulted in the highest magnitude of "missed the earnings forecast"); Quintile 5 consisted of companies with the most pessimistic consensus forecasts (i.e., the forecasts that, if unchanged, would have resulted in the highest magnitude of "beat the earnings forecast"). Figure 8.2 shows the patterns of the median earnings surprises by quintile, where the amount of the surprise is based on analyst forecasts before management guidance (Point A), managers' forecasts (Point B), and analysts' updated forecasts (Point C). Figure 8.2 illustrates four important patterns:

- The earnings surprise is closer to zero for all groups when calculated on the basis of the management forecast than when calculated on the basis of the analysts' prior forecast. Therefore, management forecasts are more accurate than analyst forecasts made prior to the management guidance.
- Analysts' forecasts made posterior to the management guidance mirror management forecasts. So, analysts are using the information in management forecasts to revise their forecasts.
- The change between the surprise based on managers' forecasts (Point B) and the surprise based on the analysts' posterior forecasts (Point C) is greatest for Quintile 1. Therefore, adjustments to analysts' forecasts are greatest for the most optimistic forecasts.
- The change between analysts' prior forecasts (Point A) and managers' forecasts (Point B) is smaller for Quintiles 4 and 5 than for Quintiles 1–3. So, managers appear to correct pessimistic forecasts (Quintiles 4 and 5) to a lesser degree than optimistic forecasts.

---

[42]Kasznik pointed out that an alternative interpretation is that an abnormal level of accruals motivates the issuance of an optimistic forecast.

©2004, The Research Foundation of CFA Institute

Figure 8.2.   Effect of Management EPS Forecasts on Analyst Forecasts, 1994–2003

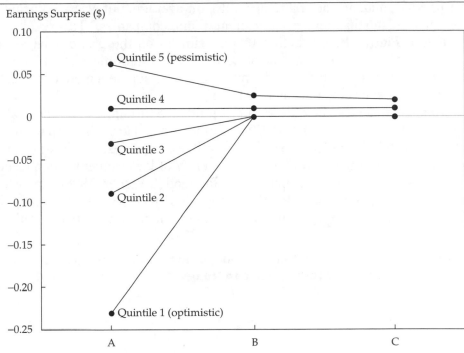

A = Surprise Based on Analyst Forecasts before Management Guidance
B = Surprise Based on Management Forecast   C = Analyst Posterior Forecast

Note: Sample consisted of 2,724 company-quarters. Companies were ranked into five portfolios on the basis of the amount of the earnings surprise, calculated by using analyst forecasts before management guidance to measure forecasted earnings. These five portfolios were then followed through time. Point B is the earnings surprise for each of the five portfolios based on management forecasts. Point C is the earnings surprise for each of the five portfolios based on analysts' posterior forecasts. The earnings surprise is measured as actual EPS minus forecasted EPS.
Source: Feng (2003)

Other Management Guidance and Forecast Accuracy

Forecasts of earnings are only one type of guidance that corporate managers can provide. Prior to Reg FD, guidance could include appropriate earnings models. Hutton (2003) analyzed data from a 2001 National Investor Relations Institute survey that asked the question: "Do you review analyst earnings models?" There were 457 companies that said yes and 59 companies that provided no guidance. Hutton found that companies that provide guidance ("guiding companies") are the larger companies that have higher market-to-book ratios, have more institutional holdings, and have a greater analyst following. Hutton found that the consensus analyst forecasts for companies that provide guidance are more accurate, on average, but also significantly more pessimistic than forecasts for "nonguiding companies." This result can be seen in **Figure 8.3**. Whether this pessimism on the part of analysts is unintentional or an intentional payback for being in the "information loop" is unclear. But the benefit to the company is clear: Management guidance makes it easier to meet or beat the consensus forecast.

Managers can also provide earnings guidance through conference calls. Frankel, Johnson, and Skinner (1999) documented that growth companies are more likely to hold conference calls than other companies, possibly because the growth companies' earnings are inherently of lower quality when calculated by using the current financial reporting model. Tasker (1998) supported this conjecture; she documented that companies that choose to use quarterly conference calls to convey information are more likely to have poor earnings

Figure 8.3. Deviations of Actual Earnings from Consensus Analyst Forecasts for Guiding and Nonguiding Companies, 2001

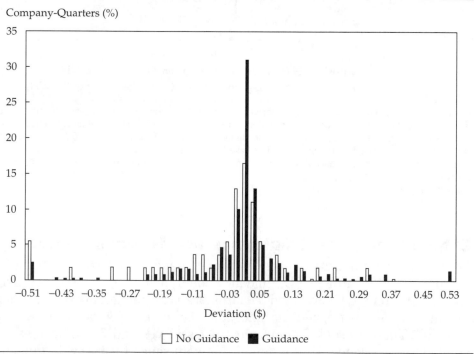

Note: Deviations calculated as actual earnings per share minus forecasted earnings per share.
Source: Hutton (2003).

©2004, The Research Foundation of CFA Institute

quality. Frankel, Johnson, and Skinner documented unusually large return volatility and trading volume at the time of a call, which suggests that conference calls convey information. Bowen, Davis, and Matsumoto (2002) found that conference calls reduce the dispersion in analysts' forecasts. They also found that the weaker analysts (i.e., those with the worst prior forecasting ability) benefited most from the conference call. These papers suggest that managers voluntarily supplement required disclosures with informative voluntary disclosures in conference calls.

Further research on open versus closed conference calls can help answer the question noted earlier of whether requiring more open disclosure is beneficial to all market participants. Requirements for open disclosure may level the playing field among investors, but they may also create incentives to reduce information gathering, resulting in less total information availability.

The requirements will also have adverse market consequences if unsophisticated investors do not properly interpret the information but attempt to trade on it.[43] Bushee, Matsumoto, and Miller (2003) provided evidence of higher stock price volatility and individual investor trading during open conference calls relative to closed calls. Their evidence is consistent with the perspective that open calls encourage trading by relatively uninformed investors. These investors remain relatively uninformed despite the call, but they appear to increase their trading activity, presumably as a result of feeling more informed.

Effects of Regulation Fair Disclosure

Reg FD, which went into effect on 23 October 2000, prohibits managers from providing material information to selected investors or analysts without simultaneously releasing the information to the public. Two significant anticipated benefits of Reg FD are (1) an increase in the integrity of capital markets because the ability of a few investors to profit at the expense of others will be limited and (2) an increase in the independence of analysts, who will no longer be cut out of the "information loop" if they write an unfavorable report. But Reg FD could be costly to the analyst and investor communities. Some have argued that Reg FD could result in a decrease in the amount of information available about companies for three reasons:

- Managers may be unwilling to disclose proprietary or sensitive information to the public that they would have disclosed privately to analysts.

---

[43]See Skinner (2003) for an excellent discussion of these issues, in particular in the context of conference calls.

- Uncertainty about information content may increase because media reporters and editors, who lack analysts' expertise and experience, are among the first to see and interpret financial information.
- Managers may be less forthcoming in their disclosures because of fears of misinterpretation and litigation.

Several researchers have examined the implications of Reg FD for earnings quality. In all cases, based on comparisons of the pre– and post–Reg FD periods, the researchers have concluded that Reg FD has not had a material effect on the total information that is available about companies.

Two papers directly examined changes in disclosure proclivity around the implementation of Reg FD. Bushee et al. documented that Reg FD had only a small impact on companies' decisions to hold conference calls. Some companies did discontinue hosting conference calls after Reg FD, but they were companies that the study identified as gaining little benefit from hosting calls. The study also indicated that Reg FD did not limit the amount of information disclosed during conference calls. The authors concluded that Reg FD did not hurt companies' information environments, on average, despite some evidence of an increase in stock price volatility and individual investor trading during conference calls after Reg FD. Shane, Soderstrom, and Yoon (2001) documented an increase in managers' voluntary public disclosures after Reg FD. They also concluded that Reg FD did not weaken the overall information environment of their sample companies, on average.

Two other papers examined capital market effects around the implementation of Reg FD to infer its effect on information availability. Heflin, Subramanyam, and Zhang (2003) compared various information-related characteristics of the post–Reg FD period (the fourth quarter of 2000 and the first and second quarters of 2001) and the pre–Reg FD periods (the analogous quarters in the prior year). For a sample of 2,025 companies, they found that the average analyst forecast error (absolute value) was larger in the post–Reg FD period and the dispersion of forecasts was greater. Further evidence indicates, however, that this finding is attributable to a change in the economic environment (decline in the economy) rather than Reg FD. They also documented that stock price reactions to earnings announcements are smaller since the implementation of Reg FD. The authors conclude that since Reg FD, companies are releasing more information prior to earnings announcements than they were before Reg FD. Eleswarapu, Thompson, and Venkataraman (forthcoming 2004) and Lee, Rosenthal, and Gleason (2004) found that liquidity and trading costs did not change after Reg FD. An important aspect of the Eleswarapu et al. study is that their finding held for companies of different sizes. Their study does not support concerns that Reg FD would impose hardships on small companies by making it more difficult for them to attract analyst coverage.

Overall, the evidence suggests that not many changes occurred in information availability after Reg FD. But two caveats are in order. First, Reg FD is not the only significant event that occurred in the 2000–01 time period. Reg FD came about, at least in part, because investors had started to question, more than ever before, the integrity of the U.S. capital markets. Thus, comparisons of the pre– and post–Reg FD periods may not be able to capture the effects of Reg FD alone. Second, the results are based on a fairly short sample period; the long-term effects of Reg FD obviously cannot yet be evaluated. Researchers have begun to measure the intended effects of Reg FD, but unintended consequences affecting information availability and earnings quality will also surely occur.

One potential unintended consequence of Reg FD is that it will cause a decrease in analysis of financial information. We hope the evidence presented in this monograph has made clear that analysts play a crucial role as information intermediaries—interpreting and communicating information—between a company and the capital markets. With the coming of Reg FD and other structural changes in the industry related to the separation of analysis and banking activities, the incentives to serve this vital role as intermediary may decrease and the costs associated with providing information, including administrative and expected legal costs, may increase. If analysts are forced to decrease coverage or reduce the "content" of their analyses, an unintended and costly consequence of Reg FD could very well be that the average investor has less information on which to base decisions.

9. Earnings Quality over Time

It probably comes as no surprise to the reader that various researchers have claimed that a decline in earnings quality or earnings "relevance" has been going on for the past 20 (even 40) years. These studies reached this conclusion by documenting a decline in the association between stock prices and earnings (or returns and earnings changes) over time. Panel A of **Figure 9.1** illustrates the decline by showing the association between earnings and stock returns from 1952 through 1994. Given our definition of earnings quality—that higher-quality earnings accurately annuitize the intrinsic value of the company—and assuming that market values are a good proxy for intrinsic firm values, the decline in the relationship between earnings and stock returns can be viewed as a decline in earnings quality.

Two published studies have reported that the decline in the relevance of earnings on the income statement is concurrent with an increase in the relevance of book value of equity on the balance sheet, with a net increase in the combined value relevance of the financial statements (Collins, Maydew, and Weiss 1997; Francis and Schipper 1999). Panel B of Figure 9.1 illustrates the increase in the relevance of book value of equity from 1952 through 1994.

Lev and Zarowin (1999), however, reported a decline in the relevance of both earnings and book values. The difference between their results and those of Collins, Maydew, and Weiss and of Francis and Schipper is a result of the time periods examined. The decrease in the Lev and Zarowin study occurred from 1978 through 1996, whereas the increase that the other studies reported was based on data from the past 40 years.[44]

A concern with these studies is the underlying assumption that stock prices represent intrinsic value—or at least that the association between stock price and intrinsic value has been relatively constant through time. If market prices, and thus returns, are reflecting a "bubble," then a decrease in the association between earnings and returns does not necessarily indicate

---

[44]Some controversy surrounds the interpretation of the results from all three studies. First, subsequent studies (e.g., Brown, Lo, and Lys 1999; Chang 1999) questioned the statistical validity of the results related to the book value of equity and stock prices because of scale effects. After controlling for scale effects and other econometric issues, the authors of the critiques documented a decline in the relevance of both earnings and the book value of equity. There is further disagreement about whether the subperiod results that are interpreted as indicating lower earnings quality in the late 1990s are really statistically different from earlier subperiods (Core, Guay, and Van Buskirk 2003).

Figure 9.1. Relationships between Market Data and Financial Statement Data over Time, 1952–94

A. Stock Returns and Earnings

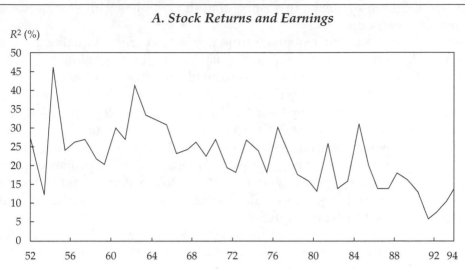

B. Market Value and Balance Sheet

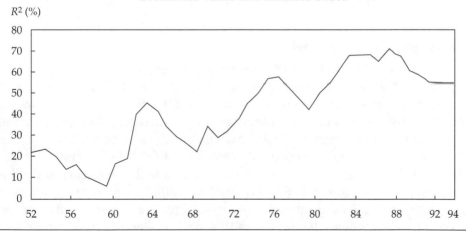

Notes: The sample was all company-year observations with data for 1952–1994 available in the Center for Research in Security Prices and Compustat files. Data range from 377 in 1952 to 4,493 in 1994. The R^2's for Panel A were obtained from the following regression run each year: $\text{Return}_j = \alpha + \beta_1\Delta\text{Earnings}_j + \beta_2\text{Earnings}_j + \epsilon_j$, where returns are cumulative market-adjusted returns for a 15-month period ending 3 months after the fiscal year-end and earnings are before extraordinary items. Earnings_j is company j's earnings before extraordinary items, deflated by the market value of equity at the beginning of the year. For Panel B, the R^2's were obtained from the following regression run each year: Market value per share$_j$ = $\alpha + \delta_1\Delta\text{Assets}_j + \delta_2\text{Liabilities}_j + \epsilon_j$, where market value per share was measured at the fiscal year-end. Assets and liabilities are on a per share basis measured at the fiscal year-end.

Source: Francis and Schipper (1999).

lower-quality earnings. The decrease could also be driven by a decline in the ability of stock prices to reflect fundamental value. Penman (2003) pointed out that valid reasons exist to suspect that the fault lies with stock returns rather than earnings.

We discuss two explanations for the decline in earnings quality as measured by its association with stock returns. The first explanation is that the nature of company operations has changed and that generally accepted accounting principles (GAAP) have not kept up with the times. In particular, more companies are reporting losses and special items. Collins, Maydew, and Weiss found that the decrease in the value relevance of earnings is associated with an increase in the frequency and magnitude of one-time items and an increase in the frequency of negative earnings. The second explanation is that two *philosophical* changes in standard setting—to a balance sheet focus and less-principles-based (i.e., more rule-oriented) focus—have produced standards that decrease earnings quality.

Following the discussion of these explanations, we point out that the increasing occurrence of losses and nonrecurring items has given rise to the use of *pro forma* earnings, a non-GAAP earnings number. We provide evidence about the usefulness of *pro forma* earnings and also some warnings about their reliability.

Times Have Changed

In the mid- to late 1990s, practicing accountants and various researchers expressed concerns about the relevance of the financial reporting model. A popular claim was that the current model is not adequate in an economy dominated by information-based technology. U.S. GAAP, they argued, was developed for and is appropriate for manufacturing companies. These critics called into question the relevance of earnings in the "New Economy" or the "Information Age." These concerns are consistent with the observed decline in earnings relevance. The U.S. economy has shifted away from manufacturing, and the average association between earnings and the value of a company's equity has declined. In support of this view, Lev and Zarowin found that companies with increased spending on research and development between 1976 and 1995 experienced a statistically significant decline in the relationship between earnings and stock returns whereas companies with decreased R&D spending experienced an increase.

But not all of the decline can be attributed to the rise of New Economy companies. Givoly and Hayn (2000) documented that the decline in the relationship between earnings and stock returns also characterized a sample of companies that were publicly traded in the 1968–98 period. That is, older companies, which were likely to be more manufacturing based than the new companies, also experienced a decline. Two major accounting-related shifts occurred concurrently with the documented decline in earnings relevance: (1) a greater incidence of losses and conservative accounting and (2) a greater incidence of special items.

Losses and Conservative Accounting. A major change that occurred concurrently with the declining relevance of earnings is that more companies began reporting losses (Givoly and Hayn). In the 1960s, about 7 percent of companies reported losses, whereas in the 1990s, about 30 percent reported losses. Cash from operations did not follow a similar pattern; that is, the losses were mainly a result of nonoperating accruals. **Figure 9.2** illustrates these trends. Givoly and Hayn also showed that bottom-line earnings volatility has increased over time. Since 1993, earnings have become more volatile, on average, than cash flows. Matching accruals—those that reduce the volatility of earnings by counteracting the volatility in cash flows—have declined.

The fact that the frequency of losses and earnings volatility have increased may explain the decline in earnings quality, but the fundamental question remains: What has caused companies to report more losses and more volatile earnings numbers? Givoly and Hayn examined several possible explanations—structural changes in U.S. industries, the changing composition of U.S. industries toward companies with more intangible assets, the inclusion of younger companies in the databases, and a move to focus on the valuation of assets and liabilities by the Financial Accounting Standards Board (FASB) and

Figure 9.2. Frequency of Losses in Earnings vs. Cash from Operations, 1952–99

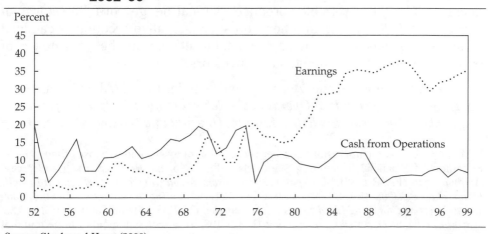

Source: Givoly and Hayn (2000).

other accounting standard setters. After examining these explanations, Givoly and Hayn concluded that, as a result of a change in the FASB's focus, accounting has become more "conservative"—defined as recognizing the full extent of losses as early as possible and deferring the recognition of gains. They suggested that the FASB's focus on the valuation of assets and liabilities has led to rules that result in a higher likelihood of large write-offs (and thus losses) and more volatile earnings streams.[45]

A move to more conservative accounting is not without negative consequences. Penman and Zhang (2002) investigated several conservative accounting rules, including the expensing of R&D and advertising costs and the use of the LIFO (last in, first out) inventory method. For a growing company, expensing R&D or advertising or using LIFO creates a "reserve" of future earnings. For example, expensing more R&D in the current period rather than capitalizing R&D depresses current earnings. The cost is reported in current earnings, whereas the sales associated with those costs are reported in future periods. As a company moves from high growth to low (or no) growth, however, the practice of expensing R&D costs when incurred generates earnings that are higher than they would be if R&D were capitalized. The prior-period investments in R&D are still generating sales, so these revenues, combined with a reduction in R&D expenses as growth declines, lead to an increase in earnings. The increase is not persistent, however, because without further investments in R&D, future sales will decline.

Penman and Zhang showed that companies with extreme changes in their LIFO reserves, R&D expenditures, and advertising expenditures have temporary distortions in their earnings. A hypothetical trading strategy that bought equity in companies with unusually large changes in these variables and sold short equity in companies with unusually small changes (i.e., decreases) in these variables produced annual hedge portfolio returns of approximately 9 percent. In other words, conservative accounting can lead to stock misvaluation when its predictable effects on the persistence of earnings are not fully understood by investors.

Special Items. Under Accounting Principles Board (APB) Opinion No. 30, *Reporting the Results of Operations—Reporting the Effects of Disposal of a Segment of a Business, and Extraordinary, Unusual and Infrequently Occurring*

---

[45] Many FASB statements result in earlier recognition of losses and expenses than gains— Statement of Financial Accounting Standards (SFAS) No. 68, *Research and Development Arrangements* (FASB 1982), SFAS No. 106, *Employers' Accounting for Postretirement Benefits Other Than Pensions* (FASB 1992a), SFAS No. 121, *Accounting for the Impairment of Long-Lived Assets and for Long-Lived Assets to Be Disposed Of* (FASB 1995a), and SFAS No. 123, *Accounting for Stock-Based Compensation* (FASB 1995b). FASB statements can be found at www.fasb.org/st/.

Events and Transactions (APB 1973), income related to events that are unusual or infrequent but not both may be reported separately on the income statement but must be reported "above the line," on a pretax basis. That is, these special items cannot be segregated on an after-tax basis, as extraordinary items can.[46] Special items may be either operating or nonoperating. Common examples of special items are restructuring charges, asset impairment charges, litigation-related losses, and merger/acquisition-related expenses.

Special items are not that special anymore. The frequency of reporting of special items has increased significantly in the past few decades, and the increase has been linked to the decline in earnings relevance (see Collins, Maydew, and Weiss; Bradshaw and Sloan 2002). **Figure 9.3** illustrates the trend in the reporting of large (greater than 1 percent of total assets) special items from 1982 through 2001. In 1982, fewer than 10 percent of U.S. companies in the Compustat database reported large special items. In 2001, more than 25 percent of companies reported large special items. Note that the trend in the reporting of special items is primarily driven by negative special items.

An important question is whether the increase in negative special items is legitimate and related to changes in how companies operate or whether it represents an increase in earnings manipulation by management. The U.S. Securities and Exchange Commission (SEC) has accused companies of trying to mislead investors by including normal persistent expenses in these "nonrecurring" charges. One method of abuse is to overstate total expenses for the period and create "hidden reserves" that can be used to hide operating expenses in later periods. For example, consider the accounting implications of overestimating costs associated with a restructuring. The company takes a restructuring charge in Year 1 and records a liability for the anticipated future costs plus some cushion. Analysts and investors consider the charge to be nonrecurring and capitalize the effect of the nonrecurring charge into stock price valuations. In Years 2–4, the company makes expenditures associated with its ongoing operations. But instead of increasing current-period expenses and decreasing current-period net income in those years, the company reduces its overstated restructuring

---

[46]"Extraordinary" treatment of an event/transaction, which means that the item is segregated and reported on an after-tax basis, is permitted only if the event is both unusual and infrequent. Such treatment is rare. *Accounting Trends and Techniques* (AICPA 2002) reported that only 78 of the 600 annual reports surveyed contained extraordinary items. Of these, 70 were related to debt extinguishments. In 2002, the FASB rescinded SFAS No. 4 (FASB 1975), so gains and losses related to early extinguishments of debt are no longer automatically treated as extraordinary. Thus, only 8 of the 600 companies surveyed (approximately 1 percent) reported items that meet the current definition of "extraordinary."

Figure 9.3. Companies Reporting Significant Special Items, 1982–2001

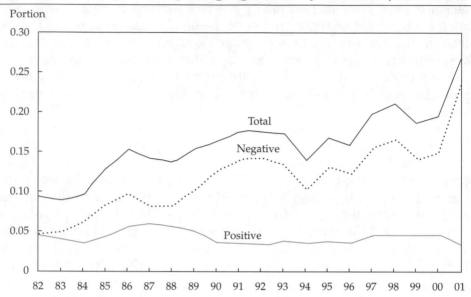

Note: This figure follows the approach of Elliott and Hanna (1986) for an earlier period.
Source: Compustat.

liability. Thus, in Years 2–4, the company overstates its operating income, which financial statement users perceive to be recurring and value at a higher capitalization rate.[47]

Another method of abuse is to simply classify recurring current-period operating expenses as special items. Thus, total income for the period is correct but the components, which should be related to persistence and valuation, are not. McVay (2003) provided evidence of this transferring type of behavior.

Borden Foods Corporation and Kimberly-Clark Corporation provide specific examples of these two types of abuses. Borden reported in a press release in 1994 that it would reverse part of its 1992 restructuring charge following "comments from and discussions with the staff of the Securities and Exchange Commission." The company reclassified $145.5 million of the $642.0 million pretax restructuring charge to operating expenses with a note that the amounts were unrelated to the restructuring and, instead, represented promotional

---

[47] Corporate compensation committees typically exclude special items such as restructuring charges from earnings when determining earnings-based bonuses for top management (see Dechow, Huson, and Sloan 1994). Thus, overstating the restructuring charge is not likely to penalize managers' compensation and could actually increase it in future years.

©2004, The Research Foundation of CFA Institute

accruals, asset write-downs, and environmental and litigation charges. An additional $119.3 million of the original charge was also reversed. Various press accounts indicated that this amount included accruals for "promotional activities" that Borden claimed were subsequently canceled. Kimberly-Clark recorded a $1.44 billion restructuring charge after its merger with Scott Paper Company in 1995. The SEC issued an official Accounting and Auditing Enforcement Release (AAER) claiming that approximately 25 percent of the charge represented merger-related expenses, not restructuring costs.

Even though the classification of recurring items as special does not affect total reported earnings, this issue is important under the assumption that investors value income statement components differently on the basis of the components' perceived persistence. Research evidence supports this assumption. Specifically, Elliott and Hanna (1996) showed that the capitalization rate of special items into stock returns is significantly lower than the capitalization rate of recurring earnings into stock returns. In other words, investors do not lower their valuations of a company when earnings are low because of a restructuring charge by as much as they do if earnings are low because of ongoing operating activities.

We address four questions related to negative special items:

1. Are the special items really nonrecurring?
2. Do managers classify negative recurring items as special to boost future earnings? In other words, are special items used as an earnings-management tool?
3. How do investors perceive the charges for special items; do they fully understand the valuation implications?
4. Will the new rules for impairment/restructuring charges improve earnings quality?

■ *Are nonrecurring charges nonrecurring?* Empirical evidence on restructuring charges and other impairment charges suggests that these nonrecurring charges typically recur. For the 1989–92 period, Francis, Hanna, and Vincent (1996) documented that the likelihood a company would take a write-off—including impairment charges on goodwill; plant, property and equipment (PP&E); or inventory and restructuring charges—was positively related to the number of charges it had taken in the previous five years and to the average number of charges taken during that period by companies in the same industry. For 1975–1994, Elliott and Hanna found that 50 percent of companies that took one write-off went on to take a second within 12 quarters. Half of those went on to take a third write-off, and 6 percent of their sample companies that took at least one write-off eventually took more than four in the subsequent 12-quarter period. These patterns cast doubt on the notion that negative special items are nonrecurring.

The financial press has noted this problem. A 2002 *Fortune* magazine article about Eastman Kodak Company stated, "The company has recorded 'nonrecurring' losses in ten of the past 12 years" (Serwer 2002, p. 147).

■ *Are special items an earnings-management tool?* Several papers have provided evidence that is consistent with the use of special items for earnings management. Moehrle (2002) investigated companies that reversed restructuring accruals, an action that implies that the original accrual was an overestimate. He found that companies were more likely to reverse previously recorded charges when earnings without the reversal would have fallen short of analyst forecasts or when earnings before the reversal were negative. These results suggest that managers create reserves at the time of the restructuring charge that are used to hide operating expenses in later periods.

Francis, Hanna, and Vincent provided two pieces of evidence that are consistent with a strategic element to the timing of special charges. First, they documented that write-offs follow poor abnormal stock return performance. Second, they found that key management changes occur concurrently with goodwill write-offs, PP&E write-offs, and restructuring charges but not with inventory write-offs. An explanation for this result [one offered by Pourciau (1993) and others] is that new managers can blame the old managers for the poor performance and "clear the decks" to increase their chances of good future performance. Inventory write-offs are different because managers have less discretion over the timing of inventory write-offs than other write-offs.

Myers (2001) suggested that managers time restructuring charges to smooth income when earnings are high or to take a bath when earnings are low. Companies are more likely to take a restructuring charge when managers can use the hidden reserves to manipulate earnings to increase compensation bonuses in future years. In Myers' study, the composition of the board of directors with respect to inside versus outside directors did not affect the amount of discretion in the charges, but a high-quality audit committee (of at least three independent members, at least one of whom had accounting or related financial expertise) did. Her evidence suggests, again, that managers are acting strategically; when able, they record special items to manage earnings.

In summary, an analyst should carefully consider the implications of nonrecurring charges for earnings persistence when (1) a new management team records nonrecurring charges, (2) the company has taken a charge before, and/or (3) the company has poor prior return performance. These situations are all indicators that the nonrecurring charge, specifically if it involves estimation and judgment, is likely to contain a "managed" element.

■ *How do investors value special items?* Francis, Hanna, and Vincent found that the market reaction to write-off announcements during their sample period (1989–1992) was negative. For every 1 percent of assets written off, the company had an excess return of –0.08 in the two-day period surrounding the announcement of the write-off. The stock price reaction varied, however, by the write-off type: It was negative for inventory write-offs, zero for goodwill and PP&E write-offs, and positive for restructuring charges. The authors suggested that inventory write-offs convey information only about asset value impairment but the other types of charges convey information about future company activities. If the market views the future activities as positive, one would expect positive effects countervailing the negative effects of impairment news.

Elliott and Hanna showed that investors react more negatively to special items if the company has taken such charges repeatedly. In addition, the stock price response to the earnings that exclude the special item is weaker. The authors interpreted this result as evidence that the market is increasingly suspicious of the earnings persistence for companies with recurring "nonrecurring" items.

Burgstahler, Jiambalvo, and Shevlin (2002) also suggested that investors are fairly sophisticated with respect to pricing special items, but their results indicate that investors do not *fully* understand the implications of special items. The authors reported statistically significant, although economically small, abnormal returns in a three-day window around companies' earnings announcements for a hypothetical hedge portfolio. The portfolio consisted of a long position in companies that reported negative special items four quarters prior to portfolio formation and a short position in companies that reported positive special items four quarters prior. Positive nonrecurring items were, on average, followed by *positive* earnings. But negative special items were also followed by *positive* earnings, which the authors suggested is consistent with a shifting of future costs to the current period. The positive hedge returns indicate that investors underestimated the persistence of positive special items and/or overestimated the persistence of negative special items.

■ *Will the new rules improve earnings quality?* In the summer of 2002, the FASB issued SFAS No. 146, *Accounting for Costs Associated with Exit or Disposal Activities* (FASB 2002), to be effective for disposals and exit activities initiated after 31 December 2002. The standard provides detailed guidance on the types of charges that can be included in a restructuring charge. This additional guidance will improve earnings quality if it effectively restricts a company's ability to classify recurring operating expenses as nonrecurring, special items.

The new standard has two key provisions that will differentiate current restructuring charges from those taken in the past. First, all costs are to be measured at fair value (i.e., the present value of future cash flows). If a fair value cannot be determined, the company should wait to recognize the obligation until a fair value can be determined. Second, a "liability" for future costs cannot be recognized until the company has incurred a liability as that term is generally defined in the accounting standards. The FASB provides detailed guidance on conditions associated with restructurings that imply when a liability has been incurred, and these conditions are more restrictive than practice prior to SFAS No. 146.[48] Most notably, anticipated future operating losses cannot be accrued as a liability. This change is likely to increase the frequency of losses reported in the future, making it even more important than in the past for analysts to understand and interpret special items.

Philosophical Changes in Standard Setting

A second explanation for the decline in earnings quality is that recent accounting standards have a different underlying philosophy of "earnings quality" from that of standards written in the 1950s and 1960s. We discuss two ways in which the standards have changed through time and the impact of these changes on earnings quality. First, recent standards increasingly reflect a balance sheet perspective and focus on fair value accounting. Second, recent standards tend to be more rule oriented and less principles based.

Balance Sheet Perspective. Statement of Financial Accounting Concepts No. 1 enumerates the FASB's stated objectives for financial reporting, which provide the foundation for its standards. The objectives are as follows (italics added):

- Financial reporting should provide information that is useful to present and potential investors and creditors and other users in making rational investment, credit, and similar decisions. The information should be comprehensible to those who have a reasonable understanding of business and economic activities and are willing to study the information with reasonable diligence.

---

[48]For example, related to one-time termination benefits, a company can recognize a liability only when it has an appropriately approved termination plan that specifies (1) the number of employees that will be terminated and their job classifications, (2) the expected completion date of the plan, and (3) the detailed terms of the termination benefits. Related to the costs associated with early termination of a contract, the company records a liability at fair value (i.e., the present value of future cash flows) when the company terminates the contract in accordance with the contract terms, which may be after the plan commitment date if the restructured operations are to be phased out over a period. For the company to recognize a termination liability, withdrawal or significant alteration of the plan must be unlikely.

- Financial reporting should *provide information to help present and potential investors and creditors and other users in assessing the amounts, timing, and uncertainty of prospective cash receipts* from dividends or interest and the proceeds from the sale, redemption, or maturity of securities or loans. Since investors' and creditors' cash flows are related to enterprise cash flows, financial reporting should provide information to help investors, creditors, and others assess the amounts, timing, and uncertainty of prospective net cash inflows to the related enterprise.
- Financial reporting should *provide information about the economic resources of an enterprise, the claims to those resources* (obligations of the enterprise to transfer resources to other entities and owners' equity), and the effects of transactions, events, and circumstances that change its resources and claims to those resources. (FASB 1978, p. 5)

The second and third objectives can produce a conflict for standard setters. A standard may provide useful information about current operations and their ability to generate cash flows, but it may do so by distorting numbers reported on the balance sheet. For example, capitalizing software development costs and expensing them as the software is sold may provide a good indication of the profit margin for a software company. The capitalized software development costs reported as an asset, however, may not reflect the "fair value" of that asset (i.e., the price for which the undeveloped software could be sold to an independent third party). Similarly, a focus on reporting assets and liabilities at fair value can lead to adjusting entries that distort earnings. Changes in balance sheet accounts have to be recorded somewhere. If these transitory valuation adjustments are forced through earnings, the impact may be a decrease in the information that earnings provide to predict future cash flows.

In recent years, the FASB has adopted a balance sheet perspective and focused on meeting its objective to provide information about an enterprise's resources and obligations.[49] Consider, for example, the accounting for income taxes. Under APB Opinion No. 11, *Accounting for Income Taxes* (APB 1967), the predecessor standard to the current rules, the income tax provision on the income statement was basically equal to pretax income recognized during the current year under GAAP, regardless of when it would be recognized for tax purposes, multiplied by the current tax rate. Deferred tax assets (DTAs) and deferred tax liabilities (DTLs) on the balance sheet were

---

[49]Storey and Storey (1998) provide a very readable summary of the history of the accounting rule-making process and the changes in its focus from the 1930s to the present. The authors also describe the tension between focusing on the matching principle and the periodic reporting of income and focusing on the balance sheet. A colorful description in the monograph shows that the focus on the income statement results in a balance sheet that contains assets, liabilities, and "what-you-may-call-its," which are deferred credits or deferred charges necessary to achieve proper matching of periodic income (attributed to Robert T. Sprouse).

adjusted each period to reflect the difference between the current-year tax provision (as defined in APB No. 11) and the company's current-year tax obligation based on its actual taxable income.[50]

The current income tax accounting standard (SFAS No. 109, *Accounting for Income Taxes*; see FASB 1992b) explicitly states that the rules require "an asset and liability approach for financial accounting and reporting for income taxes" with a focus on reporting the correct obligation to tax authorities. Companies determine DTAs and DTLs associated with existing temporary differences by using current tax rates, and they record valuation allowances, if necessary, against DTAs. The provision for income taxes includes the current-period consequences of differences between GAAP and tax reporting, as in the pre–SFAS No. 109 period, but it also includes the effects of changes in estimates affecting the DTA and DTL balances, such as changes in tax rates and adjustments to the valuation allowance.[51] The latter adjustments add noise to the tax expense recorded in earnings and distort estimates of the company's effective tax rate, but the balance sheet amounts (DTLs and DTAs) in post–SFAS No. 109 financial statements represent an "obligation" or an "economic resource" in a more meaningful way than they did under APB No. 11.

Several other examples of accounting rules that reflect the FASB's focus on appropriate accounting for balance sheet items rather than earnings are as follows:

- marking to market of marketable securities,
- computing pension liabilities,
- marking to market of derivatives,
- recording asset impairments/restructuring charges,
- amortizing goodwill and applying the new impairment tests, and
- asset securitizations.

Schipper and Vincent (2003) discussed the effect on earnings of moving to fair value accounting for assets and liabilities. They pointed out that earnings will be closer to a "Hicksian" definition of income—that is, income measures the change in wealth between two periods. By definition, the change

---

[50]DTAs and DTLs were not adjusted to reflect changes in estimates of the tax consequences of differences between GAAP and tax reporting or to reflect the consequences of changes in tax rates.

[51]Prior to the accounting change, U.S. federal corporate income tax rates had been as high as 46 percent. DTAs and DTLs were created at these rates and left unadjusted. At the time of the change, tax rates were 34 percent. Companies that were in a net DTL position, which included most companies, recorded a one-time earnings benefit and reduced their net tax-related liabilities to reflect the lower rates. The change in the measurement of DTAs and DTLs was significant in dollar terms. IBM Corporation, for example, recorded a $1.9 billion benefit in 1992, which represented 28 percent of its earnings per share. Citicorp recorded a benefit of $300 million, or 18 percent of earnings per share.

in wealth is unpredictable, and analysts should expect to see losses as frequently as profits when fair value rules are applied to more assets and liabilities on companies' books. This pattern was visible in Figure 9.2.

The FASB recognizes the tension between its objective to develop a financial reporting system that faithfully represents a company's assets, liabilities, and equity claims and its objective to provide information that is useful for assessing future cash flows. The concept of "other comprehensive income" (OCI) is a direct result of this tension; it reflects the FASB's attempt to preserve the informativeness of earnings about cash flows while maintaining a focus on the balance sheet. OCI includes adjustments related to available-for-sale marketable securities, pension obligations, certain derivatives gains and losses, and certain foreign exchange gains and losses. The first three of these items (available-for-sale marketable securities, pension obligations, and certain derivatives gains and losses) correspond to the first three bullet points in the previous list of balance sheet–focused standards. Thus, while maintaining its focus on the balance sheet, the FASB has not forced the associated changes in some balance sheet accounts through net income; they flow through OCI instead.

Less-Principles-Based Standards. A second change in standard setting that is concurrent with the decline in earnings quality is the increase in detailed rules that specify "bright-line" criteria that companies must meet to use a particular accounting treatment. Bright-line rules allow transactions that are economically similar but vary slightly with respect to one feature (e.g., 74 percent or 76 percent of the leased asset's useful life) to be accounted for in very different ways. The exact point at which the line is drawn is arbitrary and does not necessarily capture the intent or complexities of different transactions.

The impact on earnings quality of detailed rules rather than principles-based standards is difficult to assess. A potential benefit of bright-line rules is that they reduce managers' discretion, which might, in turn, reduce some forms of earnings management. However, they also allow companies to engage in a particular type of earnings management: Company managers can structure transactions that just meet the bright-line requirement and achieve a particular accounting treatment without any regard for the intent of the standard. The company can hide behind the rule to defend itself against claims of fraudulent accounting.

In addition, managers can use the flexibility inherent in principles-based standards, together with their knowledge about the company, to increase earnings quality by choosing accounting procedures that produce earnings data that best reflect the underlying economics of the company. Or managers can abuse the flexibility and decrease earnings quality. Clearly, the quality of corporate governance and monitoring of financial reporting will have a significant impact on whether principles-based standards result in higher-quality earnings. When managers focus too heavily on meeting quarterly forecasts, when boards of directors have little financial expertise or their positions hinge on pleasing the chief executive officer, or when auditors do not act independently, no system of accounting is likely to produce high-quality earnings.

The FASB has recently issued a proposal to move toward a more principles-based approach to standard setting. The SEC also is assessing more principles-based standards, partly because of requirements in the Sarbanes–Oxley Act that it do so. Such a fundamental change in standard setting will not occur, however, in the short term.

In summary, the decline in the association between earnings and stock returns is well documented, but no single culprit is to blame. Changes in the nature of U.S. companies' operations and changes in standard setting occurred concurrently with the decline. Both changes appear to be at least partly responsible for the decline. Other possible explanations for the decline, explanations that are not well researched, are changes in corporate governance and changes in the roles that analysts and investment banks play in the stock market. Finally, overconfidence in the stock market at various periods in the recent past may have led investors to ignore important signals revealed in the financial statements.

The Rise of *Pro Forma* Earnings

The reporting of *pro forma* earnings is a phenomenon that exploded in the late 1990s. There is no formal definition of *pro forma* earnings; it is a non-GAAP measure of performance and thus effectively allows for unlimited discretion in its determination. The flexibility can be used in two ways. On the one hand, managers can use the flexibility to report an earnings figure that is better than GAAP earnings as a measure of recurring earnings or "permanent" earnings. On the other hand, managers can use the flexibility to opportunistically influence the market's perception of the company's recurring earnings.

How useful are *pro forma* earnings? The issue is whether the reported *pro forma* number is, in fact, a better representation of value-relevant earnings (because irrelevant items are excluded) than GAAP earnings or whether it is misleading because it excludes value-relevant items. Bhattacharya, Black, Christensen, and Larson (2003) reported the types of expenses excluded from earnings for a sample of 1,149 press releases that contained *pro forma* earnings numbers issued between January 1998 and December 2000. **Figure 9.4** indicates that depreciation/amortization and stock compensation costs are frequently excluded items. The justification for excluding these costs is not that they are nonrecurring (they are clearly recurring items) but that they are noncash. *Pro forma* earnings data also frequently exclude R&D costs and purchased-R&D write-offs. Companies can justify excluding the cost of purchased R&D as a nonrecurring item, but R&D is likely to be recurring. The remaining excluded items that were specifically identified do appear to represent nonrecurring items, and this finding is supported by more formal evidence in Brown and Sivakumar (2001).

Figure 9.4.   Items Excluded from *Pro Forma* Earnings, 1998–2000

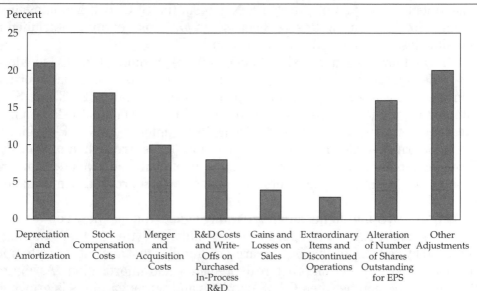

Note: The sample was those companies for which the quarterly diluted *pro forma* EPS figure differed from GAAP diluted EPS.
Source: Bhattacharya, Black, Christensen, and Larson (2003).

The observed exclusions do not indicate that managers' primary objectives are to create an earnings number that is better than GAAP earnings as a measure of recurring earnings. Depreciation, R&D, and stock compensation costs, which accounted for 46 percent of the adjustments made to GAAP earnings in Bhattacharya et al., are typically normal, recurring costs of running a business. Companies need to make ongoing investments in PP&E (depreciable assets), and the expected cash outflows associated with these investments affect company value. Depreciation, which represents the annual allocation of prior cash outflows, is one estimate of this cost. Excluding depreciation from earnings makes sense if the manager thinks that depreciation is a bad estimate of the cash flows associated with ongoing investments. But if that is the case, the manager could voluntarily provide a better estimate of annual cash outlays for PP&E—a substitute for GAAP depreciation. Such reporting has not been observed. How does excluding depreciation and amortization—an amount that is easily recognizable in the financial statements and an amount that is clearly recurring—provide value-relevant information?

The SEC has become increasingly active in pursuing companies it believes intentionally mislead investors through their *pro forma* earnings adjustments. For example, in AAER No. 1499, the SEC took action against Trump Hotels & Casino Resorts because its *pro forma* earnings excluded a one-time loss but included a one-time gain.[52]

In addition, Sarbanes–Oxley [Section 401(b)] requires the SEC to adopt new rules that address how companies report non-GAAP financial information, including *pro forma* earnings. In response, in January 2003, the SEC adopted Regulation G, which allows companies to report non-GAAP earnings but requires a reconciliation of the non-GAAP amount to GAAP earnings. Thus, Sarbanes–Oxley makes exclusions more transparent than previously. But whether such transparency will change what managers exclude from *pro forma* earnings and how investors and analysts will interpret the information is not clear.

Figure 9.5 highlights another earnings gap—the gap between "Street" earnings and GAAP earnings. Street earnings are the "actual" earnings reported by I/B/E/S—that is, the earnings number that analysts are attempting to forecast (e.g., earnings before depreciation and amortization). As Figure 9.5 shows, the gap between GAAP earnings and Street earnings is growing. Two patterns are notable in the difference: It is greatest in the fourth quarter, and it tends to be negative (excluded items are expenses). The fact that losses and special items have increased over time is probably the main reason for the growth in reporting *pro forma* earnings.

Figure 9.6 uses the Bhattacharya et al. sample to illustrate some additional patterns in *pro forma* earnings. Figure 9.6 compares *pro forma* earnings,

---

[52]The SEC stated, "In fact, had the one-time gain been excluded from the quarterly *pro forma* results as well as the one-time charge, those results would have reflected a decline in revenues and net income and would have failed to meet analysts' expectations. The undisclosed one-time gain was thus material, because it represented the difference between positive trends in revenues and earnings and negative trends in revenues and earnings, and the difference between exceeding analysts' expectations and falling short of them" (www.sec.gov/news/headlines/trumphotels.htm).

Figure 9.5.   GAAP Earnings vs. Street Earnings, 1985–97

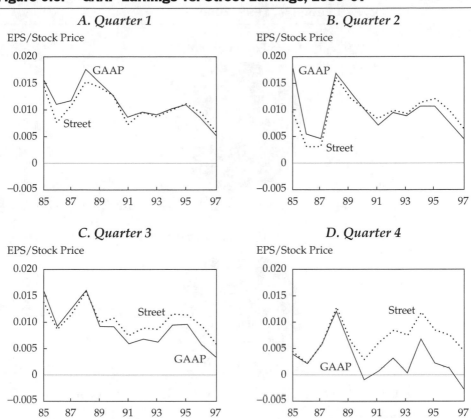

Note: GAAP earnings are earnings before extraordinary items and discontinued operations divided by average common shares outstanding (adjusted for stock splits). Street earnings are the earnings number reported by I/B/E/S, which represents earnings adjusted for certain charges considered by I/B/E/S to be nonrecurring. Earnings per share numbers are scaled by the company's stock price in the final month of its fiscal quarter-end.

Source: Bradshaw and Sloan (2002).

GAAP earnings, and earnings reported by I/B/E/S. In 70 percent of the cases, *pro forma* earnings reported in press releases are greater than GAAP earnings; I/B/E/S earnings are greater than GAAP earnings in 63 percent of the cases. As in Bradshaw and Sloan, these results indicate that most adjustments that companies and their analysts make to GAAP earnings are for negative items.

Despite these observations, several pieces of evidence taken together indicate that *pro forma* earnings can be a useful disclosure that enhances the financial reporting system. First, the earnings number that analysts forecast

Figure 9.6.   Comparisons of *Pro Forma* Earnings, GAAP Earnings, and I/B/E/S Earnings, 1998–2000

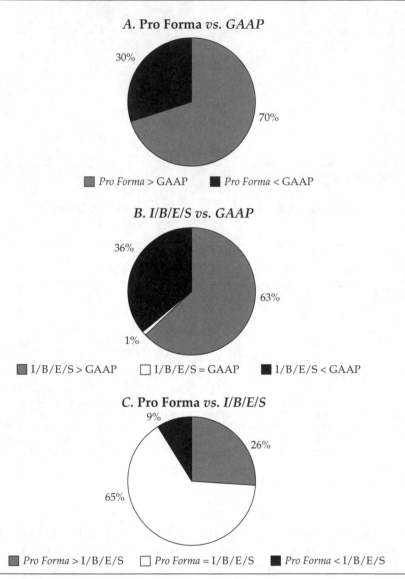

Note: See note to Figure 9.4.

Source: Bhattacharya, Black, Christensen, and Larson (2003).

(I/B/E/S earnings) excludes items that are similar to those excluded by managers in *pro forma* earnings. If analysts are trying to predict value-relevant or persistent earnings and if analysts are not excluding items because of pressure from management, this similarity suggests that *pro forma* earnings are of higher quality than GAAP earnings. Second, investors respond more strongly to the *pro forma* earnings number than to the GAAP number (Bradshaw and Sloan; Bhattacharya et al.). **Figure 9.7** illustrates that the earnings response coefficient (ERC), which was discussed in Chapter 7, has been stronger for Street earnings than for GAAP earnings, with the relative strength for Street earnings increasing throughout the 1990s. Finally, more than 40 percent of companies that reported *pro forma* earnings for quarters in 1997 through 1999 were in the business services and computer industries (Lougee and Marquardt 2002). Companies in these New Economy industries tend to have significant intangible assets, high market-to-book ratios, large sales growth, and high debt-to-equity ratios, and the current financial reporting model is not well suited to measuring the financial performance of such companies. The sample companies that reported *pro forma*

Figure 9.7. Earnings Response Coefficients, Fourth Quarter 1986–Fourth Quarter 1997

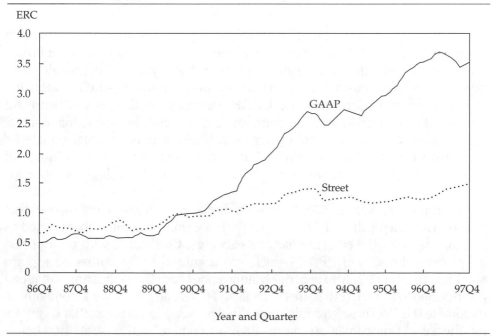

Source: Bradshaw and Sloan (2002).

earnings also had more volatile earnings, had more special items, and were more likely to be reporting losses. These characteristics suggest that companies report *pro forma* earnings when GAAP earnings are not likely to be persistent and are of low quality.

Other research, however, confirms the SEC allegations that companies use *pro forma* earnings to opportunistically influence the perceptions of investors. As Bhattacharya et al. documented, 80.1 percent of their sample companies using *pro forma* earnings beat the analyst consensus earnings forecast (see **Table 9.1**). Only 38.7 percent, however, beat the consensus

Table 9.1.   Proportion of Actual EPS that Beat or Missed the Consensus Forecast

Relation to Forecast	GAAP	I/B/E/S	*Pro Forma*
"Actual EPS" at or above mean forecast	38.7%	77.5%	80.1%
"Actual EPS" below mean forecast	61.3	22.5	19.9

Notes: "Actual EPS" is defined as GAAP, I/B/E/S, or *pro forma* earnings. See also note to Figure 9.4.

Source: Bhattacharya, Black, Christensen, and Larson (2003).

when they used GAAP earnings. One interpretation of these results is that company managers define *pro forma* earnings in order to beat analysts' forecasts. A less cynical explanation is that both analysts and companies may be appropriately focusing on the "right" earnings number—the number that is useful for valuation—and the GAAP earnings number is not the right number. Doyle, Lundholm, and Soliman (2003) found, however, that companies that report *pro forma* earnings are more likely to meet or beat the analysts' consensus forecast than companies that do not report *pro forma* earnings, and presumably analysts are forecasting the same "core" earnings number for both groups.

Schrand and Walther (2000) presented related evidence. They showed that managers strategically select the prior-period earnings amount that is used as a comparison for the current quarter's earnings. Companies with prior-period gains from the sale of PP&E, which are assumed to be nonrecurring, are significantly more likely to separately announce them than companies that had prior-period nonrecurring losses on sales. This strategy allows a company to maximize the "increase" (or minimize the decrease) in earnings that it reports for the year. Companies are more likely to engage in this strategy when it prevents a negative earnings surprise. The authors also documented that investors tend to use the benchmark provided by management to evaluate current earnings and do not adjust for the bias in managers' reporting strategies.[53]

Doyle et al. documented that managers systematically exclude from *pro forma* earnings recurring expenditures that have future cash flow implications and that investors are misled by the reporting. **Figure 9.8** shows annual returns to a hypothetical hedge portfolio that took a short position in companies in the top decile of all companies with large "total" or "other" expense exclusions and a long position in companies in the lowest decile, where the

Figure 9.8. Three-Year Returns to Hedge Portfolios Based on Total Exclusions and Other Exclusions, 1988–98

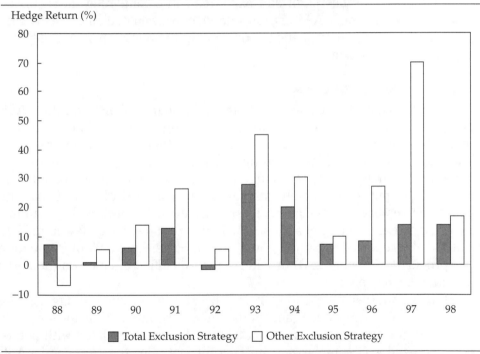

Notes: Returns are compounded buy-and-hold raw returns less the value-weighted market portfolio over a three-year period beginning two days after the quarterly earnings announcement. By calendar year. Total Exclusions = I/B/E/S EPS – GAAP EPS. Other Exclusions = I/B/E/S EPS – GAAP EPS + Special items included in GAAP EPS. The sample for which Total Exclusions did not equal zero consists of 50,132 observations in quarter *t* from 1988 through 1998.

Source: Doyle, Lundholm, and Soliman (2003).

[53]Bowen, Davis, and Matsumoto (2003) documented that companies are strategic in their reporting of *pro forma* and GAAP earnings in their press releases. Managers report the more favorable performance measure first.

portfolios were formed in each of the years 1988 through 1998.[54] Given that exclusions are typically negative, this strategy will be profitable if investors undervalue companies with low exclusions and overvalue those with high exclusions. The strategy based on "other exclusions" generated significant hedge returns of approximately 30 percent over the three-year period subsequent to the portfolio formation year. A caveat is in order, however, when extrapolating these results: The three-year return results for the portfolios formed in the later years include the time of the Internet crash, and history may not repeat itself in the future.

In summary, *pro forma* earnings tend to exclude value-irrelevant one-time components. However, investors should view *pro forma* earnings with caution. Managers also appear to use *pro forma* earnings as a marketing tool that puts the company in the best light and excludes some value-relevant recurring items. Exclusions from GAAP earnings need to be evaluated on a case-by-case basis, and the new reconciliation requirements under Sarbanes–Oxley will facilitate this evaluation.

Current Developments

Both the International Accounting Standards Board (IASB) and the FASB are working on projects to improve the reporting of financial performance. Their objective is to design a reporting system that conceptually produces a meaningful number for evaluating performance, subject to the various implementation issues. GAAP currently requires disaggregation of only three components in the income statement on an after-tax basis—extraordinary items, results from and gains/losses related to discontinued operations, and effects of accounting changes. GAAP also requires that a few items and subtotals be reported separately on a pretax basis. Rule 5-03 of Regulation S-X (provided in Appendix B) provides more specific guidance on the items that must be segregated.

Both standard-setting bodies recognize the importance of aggregating items based on persistence, and both bodies are attempting to develop a framework for aggregation based on factors that are correlated with persistence. Appendix C summarizes the current status of the IASB and FASB projects related to reporting financial performance.

---

[54]The study defined "total exclusions" as all reconciling items between GAAP earnings and *pro forma* earnings. "Other exclusions" were only those items that were not classified as special items on the income statement.

10. Summary and Conclusions

We have provided a comprehensive discussion of issues relating to earnings quality. We first described the attributes of a high-quality earnings number. Our definition focused on the primary functions of a financial analyst to forecast earnings and determine intrinsic firm value to make stock recommendations. We provided evidence that earnings are superior to cash flows along these "quality" dimensions. Earnings quality, however, varies by how well earnings are backed by cash flows. Yet, investors do not appear to be cognizant of this fact. We discussed the growing body of research that refines and extends this "accrual anomaly," and we showed how various types of accruals translate into future earnings and provide information about the persistence of earnings.

We then turned to the role of traditional techniques for financial statement analysis to assess earnings persistence and quality. Investors (and analysts) often miss important "red flags" about earnings quality that are revealed by traditional ratio analysis.

The discussion of earnings quality in the first part of the monograph emphasized that earnings quality will vary even when managers follow generally accepted accounting principles (GAAP) with the best intention of faithfully reporting earnings. In the remainder of the monograph, we focused on factors outside the financial reporting system that can affect earnings quality.

We identified the types of accounts companies are most likely to manage, through either changing their real activities or making accounting accrual adjustments. We also identified circumstances in which earnings management is most likely to occur—circumstances when analysts need to look carefully at a company's earnings quality. Research suggests that earnings management is most likely when companies are issuing equity, using equity in such transactions as mergers, or using equity as compensation. Presumably, the earnings management is done to manipulate stock prices, if only in the short run. Various types of contracts that contain earnings-based covenants or restrictions also provide incentives for earnings management. An important point of the research in this area is that companies do not always have an incentive to increase earnings. Some transactions or contracts can provide incentives to *decrease* earnings or to smooth earnings through time.

We discussed the roles various parties play in improving earnings quality. There is a link between good corporate governance structures (including effective audit committees) and earnings quality. Although it is too early to assess the impact of the Sarbanes–Oxley Act of 2002 on earnings quality, evidence suggests that if provisions that strengthen the role of the audit committee are effective, the act will improve earnings quality. Evidence also suggests that auditors can improve earnings quality, but this result is not surprising. The more important question is why auditors have not done more to improve earnings quality. Part of the reason is the definition of an auditor's role: The auditor issues an opinion only on whether the financial statements are prepared in accordance with GAAP. But as we noted throughout the first part of the monograph, GAAP does not produce an equally high-quality earnings number for all companies. Thus, a "clean" audit opinion is not equivalent to an opinion that the earnings are of high quality. Institutional investors and analysts, as sophisticated users of financial statements, also have an opportunity to be monitors of earnings quality by demanding high-quality financial statements.

We reported evidence of how investors respond to earnings data. Some have argued that greater investor response to earnings suggests that the earnings are of higher quality. We pointed out that investors do not always fully respond to information in earnings surprises. Interpretation of the evidence is difficult, however, because differences in risk and information flow among companies are not always taken into account in the studies. Nevertheless, the results generally suggest that companies with more persistent earnings generate greater investor response. The studies reveal intuitive patterns in the market's responses to earnings that provide insight into differences in earnings quality among company types.

Earnings are not the only channel available for communication about company performance. Managers can supplement the information in earnings with additional voluntary disclosures, especially when earnings quality is low. Manager "guidance" through voluntary disclosures does appear to help analysts: It improves forecast accuracy. Managers can be strategically self-serving, however, in the issuance of guidance. To evaluate the credibility of a voluntary disclosure (and the likelihood of earnings management in general), analysts need to understand managers' incentives. How much pressure does the manager have to meet next quarter's earnings forecast? What will happen to the stock price if the manager misses?

Finally, we described the decline in earnings quality through time and the major trends associated with the decline. Companies report special items and losses far more frequently now than in the past, which makes earnings more difficult to forecast. Part of this trend in reporting is legitimate; it is related to (1) an increase in "New Economy" companies, for which the accounting system does not adequately capture value, and (2) philosophical changes in standard setting that have increased the focus on the balance sheet and led to more rule-oriented standards. Part of the increased conservatism associated with reporting negative special items, however, appears to be the result of managerial manipulation. These changes require that analysts and other financial statement readers be particularly careful to assess the merits of the earnings number for predicting future earnings and cash flows. *Pro forma* earnings can make this task easier when they appropriately identify and exclude nonrecurring items from GAAP earnings. But *pro forma* earnings are also another potential tool for managers to manipulate perceptions about earnings.

What does all the research have to say about whether analysts, as a group, understand the quality of earnings? The research indicates that analysts, on average, suffer (although to a lesser extent) from biases that are similar to the biases of investors. Analysts do not fully adjust their forecasts for the differing information in cash flows and accruals, for red flags in the financial statements, or for seasonalities in quarterly earnings. Obviously, the results of the research we presented focus on averages, and there are analysts who do understand the complexities of earnings persistence and the effects of earnings quality on valuation. The goal of this monograph is to move the profession as a whole forward in better understanding the quality of earnings.

In all the discussions, we did not assume that markets are perfectly efficient and reflect all available information instantaneously and in an unbiased fashion. Research evidence shows that some stocks are mispriced in predictable ways associated with earnings quality. A careful analysis of a company's financial statements, together with an understanding of its corporate governance and the incentives its managers face, can help an analyst identify when the likelihood of earnings-quality problems is high, which is tantamount to identifying potential mispricing.

Appendix A. Trading Strategies

The various trading strategies discussed in the text are listed here, together
with the resources that provide more details on the strategies.

Basis of Trading Strategy	Resource for Details
Chapter 3	
Cash flows and accruals (measured as the difference between earnings and cash from operations)	Sloan (1996)
Discretionary accruals	Xie (2001)
Inventory accruals	Thomas and Zhang (2002); Hribar (2001)
Tax income, book income, and accruals	Hanlon (2003)
Accruals and cash flow volatility	Minton, Schrand, and Walther (2002)
Combining the accrual strategy with analyst forecasts	Barth and Hutton (2004)
Cash from operations to price	Desai, Rajgopal, and Venkatachalam (2004)
Cash flows and accruals (measured as the change in net operating assets)	Fairfield, Whisenant, and Yohn (2003b); Richardson, Sloan, Soliman, and Tuna (2003)
Cash flows from financing	Richardson and Sloan (2003)
Chapter 4	
Various fundamental ratios as signals of quality	Abarbanell and Bushee (1998)
Turnover and profit margin	Soliman (2003)
Chapter 7	
Post-earnings-announcement drift	Bernard and Thomas (1990); Joy, Litzenberger, and McEnally (1977)
Chapter 8	
Bad news forecasts by management	Soffer, Thiagarajan, and Walther (2000)
Chapter 9	
Conservative earnings strategies	Penman and Zhang (2002)
Special items and restructuring charges	Burgstahler, Jiambalvo, and Shevlin (2002)
Pro forma earnings	Doyle, Lundholm, and Soliman (2003)

Appendix B. SEC Rule 5-03: Income Statements

The U.S. Securities and Exchange Commission's Rule 5-03 specifies earnings components that should be reported as separate line items on the income statement, and it specifies required subtotals:[55]

1. Net sales and gross revenues. State separately:
   (a) net sales of tangible products,
   (b) operating revenues of public utilities or others,
   (c) income from rentals,
   (d) revenues from services, and
   (e) other revenues.
2. Costs and expenses applicable to sales and revenues. State separately the amount of:
   (a) cost of tangible goods sold,
   (b) operating expenses of public utilities or others,
   (c) expenses applicable to rental income,
   (d) cost of services, and
   (e) expenses applicable to other revenues.
3. Other operating costs and expenses. State separately any material amounts.
4. Selling, general, and administrative expenses.
5. Provision for doubtful accounts and notes.
6. Other general expenses. State separately any material item.
7. Nonoperating income. State separately in the income statement or in a note thereto:
   (a) dividends,
   (b) interest on securities,
   (c) profits on securities (net of losses), and
   (d) miscellaneous other income.
8. Interest and amortization of debt discount and expense.
9. Nonoperating expenses. State separately in the income statement or in a note thereto:
   (a) losses on securities (net of profits) and
   (b) miscellaneous income deductions.

---

[55]Excerpted from the *Coopers & Lybrand SEC Manual* (1997). The rule also contains some industry-specific guidance, which is not included here.

10. Income or loss before income tax expense and appropriate items below [that is, the rest of the numbered items].
11. Income tax expense.
12. Minority interest in income of consolidated subsidiaries.
13. Equity in earnings of unconsolidated subsidiaries and 50 percent or less owned persons.
14. Income or loss from continuing operations.
15. Discontinued operations.
16. Income or loss before extraordinary items and cumulative effects of changes in accounting principles.
17. Extraordinary items, less applicable tax.
18. Cumulative effects of changes in accounting principles.
19. Net income or loss.
20. Earnings per share data.

The reporting of unusual or infrequent items follows the guidance in Accounting Principles Board Opinion No. 30, *Reporting the Results of Operations—Reporting the Effects of Disposal of a Segment of a Business, and Extraordinary, Unusual and Infrequently Occurring Events and Transactions* (APB 1973).

Appendix C. Standard Setting on Income Statement Presentation

International Accounting Standards Board

The International Accounting Standards Board (IASB) has on its agenda a project entitled "Reporting Comprehensive Income."[56] The stated objective of the project is to address how to

> categorise and display all income and expenses for the period in a way that enhances users' understanding of the entity's achieved performance and that assists users in forming expectations of future performance.

The project proposes a prescribed format and subtotals for a comprehensive income statement, with restrictions on adding additional subtotals. Overall, the IASB appears to be unsympathetic to allowing companies to separately identify items on the income statement. In particular, in its "tentative decisions," it notes that the "extraordinary item" category should be abolished and that companies should not be allowed to report "unusual items" separately, although they can provide details about these items in the footnotes. The IASB does support separate reporting, however, of results of and gains and losses on discontinued operations.

The IASB is proposing that the income statement have four sections—business, financing, tax, and discontinued operations—with a total provided after the four sections. The more significant change is that the statement would have three columns: (1) income and expenses other than "remeasurements," (2) income and expenses resulting from revisions of prices or estimates that change the carrying value of assets and liabilities (remeasurements), and (3) a total column.

Financial Accounting Standards Board

The Financial Accounting Standards Board (FASB) has had a related project on its agenda since Fall 2001 called "Financial Performance Reporting by Business Enterprises."[57] The FASB is currently soliciting and analyzing input from users through its User Advisory Council to aid in the development of a

---

[56]See www.iasb.org.uk for the current status of IASB projects.
[57]See www.fasb.org for the current status of FASB projects.

standard. Users have confirmed that predictive ability is a key desired attribute of financial reporting, but no widespread dissatisfaction with the current reporting format has been reported. The FASB intends to monitor the progress of the IASB project, which it deems to be somewhat responsive to the FASB's needs. The FASB believes, however, that a separate FASB project is necessary now, with a goal of convergence.

The FASB's tentative conclusions indicate that it agrees with the IASB that earnings related to discontinued operations should be separate from other line items on the income statement and that extraordinary items should be abolished. The FASB proposes disaggregating items by function, although the term "function" is not yet defined. It also, like the IASB, proposes further division of the income statement, although, again, the specifics of an appropriate division have yet to be decided. Tentatively, the FASB has indicated that "financing" and "operating" items should be distinct and that "income flows" and "valuation adjustments" should be distinct.

References

Abarbanell, Jeffrey S., and Victor L. Bernard. 1992. "Tests of Analysts' Overreaction/Underreaction to Earnings Information as an Explanation for Anomalous Stock Price Behavior." *Journal of Finance*, vol. 47, no. 3 (July):1181–1207.

Abarbanell, Jeffrey S., and Brian J. Bushee. 1997. "Fundamental Analysis, Future Earnings and Stock Prices." *Journal of Accounting Research*, vol. 35, no. 1 (Spring):1–24.

———. 1998. "Abnormal Returns to a Fundamental Analysis Strategy." *Accounting Review*, vol. 73, no. 1 (January):19–45.

Abarbanell, Jeffrey S., and Reuven Lehavy. 2003. "Can Stock Recommendations Predict Earnings Forecast Errors?" *Journal of Accounting Research*, vol. 41, no. 1 (March):1–31.

Aboody, David, and Ron Kasznik. 2000. "CEO Stock Option Awards and the Timing of Corporate Voluntary Disclosures." *Journal of Accounting and Economics*, vol. 29, no. 1 (February):73–100.

Aharony, Joseph, Chan-Jane Lin, and Martin P. Loeb. 1993. "Initial Public Offerings, Accounting Choices, and Earnings Management." *Contemporary Accounting Research*, vol. 10, no. 1 (Fall):61–81.

Ahmed, Anwer S., Carolyn Takeda, and Shawn Thomas. 1999. "Bank Loan Loss Provisions: A Reexamination of Capital Management, Earnings Management, and Signaling Effects." *Journal of Accounting and Economics*, vol. 28, no. 1 (November):1–26.

AICPA. 2002. *Accounting Trends and Techniques*. 56th ed. New York: American Institute of Certified Public Accountants.

Amir, Eli, and Shlomo Benartzi. 1998. "The Assumed Rate of Return on Pension Funds and Asset Allocation as Predictors of Portfolio Performance." *Accounting Review*, vol. 73, no. 3 (July):335–352.

Amir, Eli, and Elizabeth Gordon. 1996. "Firms' Choice of Estimation Parameters: Empirical Evidence from SFAS 106." *Journal of Accounting, Auditing and Finance*, vol. 11, no. 3 (Summer):427–452.

Amir, Eli, Trevor S. Harris, and Elizabeth K. Venuti. 1993. "A Comparison of the Value-Relevance of U.S. vs. non-U.S. GAAP Accounting Measures Using Form 20-F Reconciliations." *Journal of Accounting Research*, vol. 31 (Supplement): 230–264.

APB. 1967. Opinion No. 11, *Accounting for Income Taxes*. Accounting Principles Board (December).

———. 1973. Opinion No. 30, *Reporting the Results of Operations—Reporting the Effects of Disposal of a Segment of a Business, and Extraordinary, Unusual and Infrequently Occurring Events and Transactions*. Accounting Principles Board (June).

Ball, Ray, and Philip Brown. 1968. "An Empirical Evaluation of Accounting Income Numbers." *Journal of Accounting Research*, vol. 6 (Autumn):159–178.

Ball, Ray, and Ross L. Watts. 1972. "Some Time Series Properties of Accounting Income." *Journal of Finance*, vol. 27, no. 3 (June):663–681.

Balsam, Steve, Eli Bartov, and Carol Marquardt. 2002. "Accruals Management, Investor Sophistication, and Equity Valuation: Evidence from 10-Q Filings." *Journal of Accounting Research*, vol. 40, no. 4 (September):987–1012.

Barth, Mary E., and Greg Clinch. 1996. "International Accounting Differences and Their Relation to Share Prices: Evidence from U.K., Australian, and Canadian Firms." *Contemporary Accounting Research*, vol. 13, no. 1 (Spring):135–170.

Barth, Mary E., and Amy P. Hutton. 2004. "Analyst Earnings Forecast Revisions and the Pricing of Accruals." *Review of Accounting Studies*, vol. 9, no. 1 (March):59–96.

Barth, Mary E., Donald P. Cram, and Karen K. Nelson. 2001. "Accruals and the Prediction of Future Cash Flows." *Accounting Review*, vol. 76, no. 1 (January):27–58.

Bartov, Eli. 1993. "The Timing of Asset Sales and Earnings Manipulation." *Accounting Review*, vol. 68, no. 4 (October):840–856.

Bartov, Eli, Dan Givoly, and Carla Hayn. 2002. "The Rewards to Meeting or Beating Earnings Expectations." *Journal of Accounting and Economics*, vol. 33, no. 2 (June):173–204.

Bartov, Eli, Suresh Radhakrishnan, and Itzhak Krinsky. 2000. "Investor Sophistication and Patterns in Stock Returns after Earnings Announcements." *Accounting Review*, vol. 75, no. 1 (January):55–75.

Basu, Sudipta. 1997. "The Conservatism Principle and the Asymmetric Timeliness of Earnings." *Journal of Accounting and Economics*, vol. 24, no. 1 (December):3–37.

Beasley, Mark S. 1996. "An Empirical Analysis of the Relation between the Board of Director Composition and Financial Statement Fraud." *Accounting Review*, vol. 71, no. 4 (October):443–465.

Beatty, Anne, Sandra Chamberlain, and Joseph Magliolo. 1996. "An Empirical Analysis of the Economic Implications of Fair Value Accounting for Investment Securities." *Journal of Accounting and Economics*, vol. 22, nos. 1–3 (August):43–77.

Beaver, William H. 1998. *Financial Reporting: An Accounting Revolution*. 3rd edition. Englewood Cliffs, NJ: Prentice Hall.

Beaver, William H., Maureen F. McNichols, and Karen K. Nelson. 2003. "An Alternative Interpretation of the Discontinuity in Earnings Distributions." Working paper, Stanford University.

Becker, Connie L., Mark L. DeFond, James Jiambalvo, and K.R. Subramanyam. 1998. "The Effect of Audit Quality on Earnings Management." *Contemporary Accounting Research*, vol. 15, no. 1 (Spring):1–22.

Beneish, Messod D. 1999. "Incentives and Penalties Related to Earnings Overstatements That Violate GAAP." *Accounting Review*, vol. 74, no. 4 (October):425–457.

Beneish, Messod D., and Mark E. Vargus. 2002. "Insider Trading, Earnings Quality, and Accrual Mispricing." *Accounting Review*, vol. 77, no. 4 (October):755–791.

Bernard, Victor L., and Jacob K. Thomas. 1990. "Evidence That Stock Prices Do Not Fully Reflect the Implications of Current Earnings for Future Earnings." *Journal of Accounting and Economics*, vol. 13, no. 4 (December):305–340.

Bhattacharya, Nilabhra, Ervin L. Black, Theodore E. Christensen, and Chad R. Larson. 2003. "Assessing the Relative Informativeness and Permanence of Pro Forma Earnings and GAAP Operating Earnings." *Journal of Accounting and Economics*, vol. 36, nos. 1–3 (December):285–319.

Bhojraj, Sanjeev, and Bhaskaran Swaminathan. 2003. "How Does the Corporate Bond Market Value Capital Investments and Accruals?" Working paper, Cornell University.

Biddle, Gary C., and Gim S. Seow. 1991. "The Estimation and Determinants of Associations between Returns and Earnings: Evidence from Cross-Industry Comparisons." *Journal of Accounting, Auditing and Finance*, vol. 6, no. 2 (Spring):183–232.

Black, Fischer. 1980. "The Magic in Earnings: Economic Earnings versus Accounting Earnings." *Financial Analysts Journal*, vol. 36, no. 6 (November/December):19–24.

Block, Stanley. 1999. "A Study of Financial Analysts: Practice and Theory." *Financial Analysts Journal*, vol. 55, no. 4 (July/August):86–95.

Bowen, Robert M., Angela K. Davis, and Dawn A. Matsumoto. 2002. "Do Conference Calls Affect Analysts' Forecasts?" *Accounting Review*, vol. 77, no. 2 (April):285–316.

————. 2003. "Do Firms Strategically Emphasize Performance Metrics in Their Earnings Press Releases?" Working paper, University of Washington.

Boynton, Charles E., Paul S. Dobbins, and George A. Plesko. 1992. "Earnings Management and the Corporate Alternative Minimum Tax." *Journal of Accounting Research*, vol. 30 (Supplement):131–154.

Bradshaw, Mark T., and Richard G. Sloan. 2002. "GAAP versus the Street: An Empirical Assessment of Two Alternative Definitions of Earnings." *Journal of Accounting Research*, vol. 40, no. 1 (March):41–66.

Bradshaw, Mark T., Scott A. Richardson, and Richard G. Sloan. 2001. "Do Analysts and Auditors Use Information in Accruals?" *Journal of Accounting Research*, vol. 39, no. 1 (June):45–75.

————. 2003. "Pump and Dump: An Empirical Analysis of the Relation between Corporate Financing Activities and Sell-Side Analyst Research." Working paper, University of Michigan.

Brown, Lawrence B., and Kumar N. Sivakumar. 2001. "Comparing the Quality of Three Earnings Measures." Working paper, Georgia State University.

Brown, Lawrence D., and Michael S. Rozeff. 1979. "The Predictive Value of Interim Reports for Improving Forecasts of Future Quarterly Earnings." *Accounting Review*, vol. 54, no. 3 (July):585–591.

Brown, Lawrence D., Robert L. Hagerman, Paul A. Griffin, and Mark E. Zmijewski. 1987a. "An Evaluation of Alternative Proxies for the Market's Assessment of Unexpected Earnings." *Journal of Accounting and Economics*, vol. 9, no. 2 (July):159–193.

————. 1987b. "Security Analyst Superiority Relative to Univariate Time-Series Models in Forecasting Quarterly Earnings." *Journal of Accounting and Economics*, vol. 9, no. 1 (April):61–87.

Brown, Stephen, Kin Lo, and Thomas Lys. 1999. "Use of R^2 in Accounting Research: Measuring Changes in Value Relevance over the Last Four Decades." *Journal of Accounting and Economics*, vol. 28, no. 2 (December):83–115.

Bublitz, Bruce, and Michael Ettredge. 1989. "The Information in Discretionary Outlays: Advertising, Research, and Development." *Accounting Review*, vol. 64, no. 1 (January):108–124.

Burgstahler, David C., and Ilia Dichev. 1997a. "Earnings, Adaptation and Equity Value." *Accounting Review*, vol. 72, no. 2 (April):187–215.

———. 1997b. "Earnings Management to Avoid Earnings Decreases and Losses." *Journal of Accounting and Economics*, vol. 24, no. 1 (December):99–126.

Burgstahler, David, and Michael J. Eames. 2003. "Earnings Management to Avoid Losses and Small Decreases: Are Analysts Fooled?" *Contemporary Accounting Research*, vol. 20, no. 2 (Summer):253–294.

Burgstahler, David, James Jiambalvo, and Terry Shevlin. 2002. "Do Stock Prices Fully Reflect the Implications of Special Items for Future Earnings?" *Journal of Accounting Research*, vol. 40, no. 3 (June):585–612.

Bushee, Brian J. 1998. "The Influence of Institutional Investors on Myopic R&D Investment Behavior." *Accounting Review*, vol. 73, no. 3 (July):305–333.

Bushee, Brian J., and Christopher F. Noe. 2000. "Corporate Disclosure Practices, Institutional Investors, and Stock Return Volatility." *Journal of Accounting Research*, vol. 38 (Supplement):171–202.

Bushee, Brian J., Dawn A. Matsumoto, and Gregory S. Miller. 2003. "Open versus Closed Conference Calls: The Determinants and Effects of Broadening Access to Disclosure." *Journal of Accounting and Economics*, vol. 34, nos. 1–3 (January):149–180.

Butler, Marty, Andrew J. Leone, and Michael Willenborg. 2003. "An Empirical Analysis of Auditor Reporting and Its Association with Abnormal Accruals." Working Paper No. FR 02-06, Simon Business School.

Cahan, Steven F., Betty M. Chavis, and Richard G. Elmendorf. 1997. "Earnings Management of Chemical Firms in Response to Political Costs from Environmental Legislation." *Journal of Accounting, Auditing and Finance*, vol. 12, no. 1 (Winter):37–66.

Chamberlain, Sandra, and Regina Anctil. 2003. "Determinants of the Time-Series of Earnings and Implications for Earnings Quality." Working paper, University of British Columbia.

Chang, James. 1999. "The Decline in Value Relevance of Earnings and Book Values." Working paper, University of Pennsylvania.

Chen, Peter, and Lane Daley. 1996. "Regulatory Capital, Tax, and Earnings Management Effects on Loan Loss Accruals in the Canadian Banking Industry." *Contemporary Accounting Research*, vol. 13, no. 1 (Spring):91–129.

Cheng, Qiang, and Terry Warfield. 2003. "Stock-Based Compensation, Insider Trading, and Earnings Management." Working paper, University of Wisconsin.

Choi, Sung K., and Debra C. Jeter. 1992. "The Effects of Qualified Audit Opinions on Earnings Response Coefficients." *Journal of Accounting and Economics*, vol. 15, nos. 2/3 (June–September):229–247.

Christie, Andrew A., and Jerold L. Zimmerman. 1994. "Efficient and Opportunistic Choices of Accounting Procedures: Corporate Control Contests." *Accounting Review*, vol. 69, no. 4 (October):539–566.

Collins, Daniel W., and S.P. Kothari. 1989. "An Analysis of Intertemporal and Cross-Sectional Determinants of Earnings Response Coefficients." *Journal of Accounting and Economics*, vol. 11, nos. 2/3 (July):143–181.

Collins, Daniel W., Guojin Gong, and Paul Hribar. 2003. "Investor Sophistication and the Mispricing of Accruals." *Review of Accounting Studies*, vol. 8, nos. 2/3 (June):251–276.

Collins, Daniel W., Edward L. Maydew, and Ira S. Weiss. 1997. "Changes in the Value-Relevance of Earnings and Book Values over the Past Forty Years." *Journal of Accounting and Economics*, vol. 24, no. 1 (December):39–67.

Collins, Daniel W., Morton Pincus, and Hong Xie. 1999. "Equity Valuation and Negative Earnings: The Role of Book Value of Equity." *Accounting Review*, vol. 74, no. 1 (January):29–61.

Collins, Julie H., Douglas A. Shackelford, and James Wahlen. 1995. "Bank Differences in the Coordination of Regulatory Capital, Earnings, and Taxes." *Journal of Accounting Research*, vol. 33, no. 2 (Autumn):263–291.

The Coopers & Lybrand SEC Manual. 1997. 7th ed. (Contributors: Robert H. Herz, Nelson W. Dittmar, Stephen J. Lis, William E. Decker, and Ronald J. Murray.) New York: John Wiley & Sons.

Core, John E., and Catherine M. Schrand. 1999. "The Effect of Accounting-Based Debt Covenants on Equity Valuation." *Journal of Accounting and Economics*, vol. 27, no. 1 (February):1–34.

Core, John, Wayne Guay, and Andrew Van Buskirk. 2003. "Market Valuations in the New Economy: An Investigation of What Has Changed." *Journal of Accounting and Economics*, vol. 34, nos. 1–3 (January):43–67.

Cotter, Julie, A. Irem Tuna, and Peter D. Wysocki. 2003. "Expectations Management and Beatable Targets: How Do Analysts React to Explicit Earnings Guidance?" Working paper, University of Pennsylvania.

DeAngelo, Harry, and Linda E. DeAngelo. 1991. "Union Negotiations and Corporate Policy." *Journal of Financial Economics*, vol. 30, no. 1 (November):3–43.

DeAngelo, Harry, Linda E. DeAngelo, and Douglas J. Skinner. 1994. "Accounting Choice in Troubled Companies." *Journal of Accounting and Economics*, vol. 17, nos. 1/2 (January):113–143.

DeAngelo, Linda E. 1986. "Accounting Numbers as Market Valuation Substitutes: A Study of Management Buyouts of Public Stockholders." *Accounting Review*, vol. 61, no. 3 (July):400–420.

Dechow, Patricia M. 1994. "Accounting Earnings and Cash Flows as Measures of Firm Performance: The Role of Accounting Accruals." *Journal of Accounting and Economics*, vol. 18, no. 1 (July):3–42.

Dechow, Patricia M., and Ilia D. Dichev. 2002. "The Quality of Accruals and Earnings: The Role of Accrual Estimation Errors." *Accounting Review*, vol. 77 (Supplement):35–59.

Dechow, Patricia M., and Weili Ge. 2003. "Earnings, Cash Flows, Persistence, and Growth." Working paper, University of Michigan.

Dechow, Patricia M., and Richard G. Sloan. 1991. "Executive Incentives and the Horizon Problem: An Empirical Investigation." *Journal of Accounting and Economics*, vol. 14, no. 1 (March):51–89.

———. 1997. "Returns to Contrarian Investment Strategies: Tests of Naive Expectations Hypotheses." *Journal of Financial Economics*, vol. 43, no. 1 (January):3–27.

Dechow, Patricia M., Mark Huson, and Richard Sloan. 1994. "The Effect of Restructuring Charges on Executives' Cash Compensation." *Accounting Review*, vol. 69, no. 1 (January):138–156.

Dechow, Patricia M., Amy P. Hutton, and Richard G. Sloan. 1999. "An Empirical Assessment of the Residual Income Valuation Model." *Journal of Accounting and Economics*, vol. 26, nos. 1–3 (January):1–34.

————. 2000. "The Relation between Analysts' Long-Term Earnings Forecasts and Stock Price Performance Following Equity Offerings." *Contemporary Accounting Research*, vol. 17, no. 1 (Spring):1–32.

Dechow, Patricia M., S.P. Kothari, and Ross L. Watts. 1998. "The Relation between Earnings and Cash Flows." *Journal of Accounting and Economics*, vol. 25, no. 2 (May):133–168.

Dechow, Patricia M., Scott Richardson, and Irem Tuna. 2001. "Are Benchmark Beaters Doing Anything Wrong?" Working paper, University of Michigan.

————. 2003. "Why Are Earnings Kinky? An Examination of the Earnings Management Explanation." *Review of Accounting Studies*, vol. 8, nos. 2/3 (June):355–384.

Dechow, Patricia M., Richard G. Sloan, and Amy P. Sweeney. 1995. "Detecting Earnings Management." *Accounting Review*, vol. 70, no. 2 (April):193–226.

————. 1996. "Causes and Consequences of Earnings Manipulation: An Analysis of Firms Subject to Enforcement Actions by the SEC." *Contemporary Accounting Research*, vol. 13, no. 1 (Spring):1–36.

DeFond, Mark L., and James Jiambalvo. 1993. "Factors Related to Auditor–Client Disagreements over Income-Increasing Accounting Methods." *Contemporary Accounting Research*, vol. 9, no. 2 (Spring):415–432.

————. 1994. "Debt Covenant Violation and Manipulation of Accruals." *Journal of Accounting and Economics*, vol. 17, nos. 1/2 (January):145–176.

DeFond, Mark L., and Chul W. Park. 2001. "The Reversal of Abnormal Accruals and the Market Valuation of Earnings Surprises." *Accounting Review*, vol. 76, no. 3 (July):375–404.

DeFond, Mark L., and K.R. Subramanyam. 1998. "Auditor Changes and Discretionary Accruals." *Journal of Accounting and Economics*, vol. 25, no. 1 (February):35–68.

Desai, Hemang, Shivaram Rajgopal, and Mohan Venkatachalam. "Value–Glamour and Accruals Mispricing: One Anomaly or Two?" *Accounting Review*, vol. 79, no. 2 (April):355–385.

Dhaliwal, Dan S., Cristi A. Gleason, and Lillian F. Mills. 2002. "Last Chance Earnings Management: Using Tax Expense to Achieve Earnings Targets." Working paper, University of Arizona.

Dichev, Ilia, and Douglas J. Skinner. 2002. "Large-Sample Evidence on the Debt Covenant Hypothesis." *Journal of Accounting Research*, vol. 40, no. 4 (September):1091–1123.

Doyle, Jeffrey T., and Mark T. Soliman. 2003. "Do Managers Use Pro Forma Earnings to Exceed Analyst Forecasts?" Working paper, University of Utah.

Doyle, Jeffrey T., Russell J. Lundholm, and Mark T. Soliman. 2003. "The Predictive Value of Expenses Excluded from Pro Forma Earnings." *Review of Accounting Studies*, vol. 8, nos. 2/3 (June):145–174.

DuCharme, Larry, Paul Malatesta, and Stephan Sefcik. 2001. "Earnings Management: IPO Valuation and Subsequent Performance." *Journal of Accounting, Auditing and Finance*, vol. 16, no. 4 (Fall):369–400.

Easterwood, Cintia M. 1998. "Takeovers and Incentives for Earnings Management: An Empirical Analysis." *Journal of Applied Business Research*, vol. 14, no. 1 (Winter):29–47.

Easton, Peter D., and Mark E. Zmijewski. 1989. "Cross-Sectional Variation in the Stock Market Response to Accounting Earnings Announcements." *Journal of Accounting and Economics*, vol. 11, nos. 2/3 (July):117–141.

Edwards, Edgar O., and Philip W. Bell. 1961. *The Theory and Measurement of Business Income*. Berkeley: University of California Press.

Eleswarapu, Venkat R., Rex Thompson, and Kumar Venkataraman. Forthcoming 2004. "The Impact of Regulation Fair Disclosure: Trading Costs and Information Asymmetry." *Journal of Financial and Quantitative Analysis*.

Elliott, John A., and J. Douglas Hanna. 1996. "Repeated Accounting Write-Offs and the Information Content of Earnings." *Journal of Accounting Research*, vol. 34 (Supplement):135–155.

Erickson, Merle, and Shiing-Wu Wang. 1999. "Earnings Management by Acquiring Firms in Stock for Stock Mergers." *Journal of Accounting and Economics*, vol. 27, no. 2 (April):149–176.

Ertimur, Yonca, Joshua Livnat, and M. Martikainen. 2003. "Differential Market Reactions to Revenue and Expense Surprises." *Review of Accounting Studies*, vol. 8, nos. 2/3 (June):185–211.

Fairfield, Patricia M. 1994. "P/E, B/P and the Present Value of Future Dividends." *Financial Analysts Journal*, vol. 50, no. 4 (July/August):23–31.

Fairfield, Patricia M., and Teri Lombardi Yohn. 2001. "Using Asset Turnover and Profit Margin to Forecast Changes in Profitability." *Review of Accounting Studies*, vol. 6, no. 4 (December):371–385.

Fairfield, Patricia M., Richard J. Sweeney, and Teri Lombardi Yohn. 1996. "Accounting Classification and the Predictive Content of Earnings." *Accounting Review*, vol. 71, no. 3 (July):337–355.

Fairfield, Patricia M., J. Scott Whisenant, and Teri Lombardi Yohn. 2003a. "Accrued Earnings and Growth: Implications for Future Profitability and Market Mispricing." *Accounting Review*, vol. 78, no. 1 (January):353–371.

———. 2003b. "The Differential Persistence of Accruals and Cash Flows for Future Operating Income versus Future Profitability." *Review of Accounting Studies*, vol. 8, nos. 2/3 (June):221–243.

Fama, Eugene, and Kenneth French. 1993. "Common Risk Factors in the Returns on Stocks and Bonds." *Journal of Financial Economics*, vol. 33, no. 1 (January):3–56.

FASB. 1975. Statement of Financial Accounting Standards No. 4, *Reporting Gains and Losses from Extinguishment of Debt—An Amendment of APB Opinion No. 30*. Financial Accounting Standards Board.

———. 1976. Statement of Financial Accounting Standards No. 13, *Accounting for Leases*. Financial Accounting Standards Board.

———. 1978. Concepts Statement No. 1, *Objectives of Financial Reporting by Business Enterprises*. Financial Accounting Standards Board.

———. 1982. Statement of Financial Accounting Standards No. 68, *Research and Development Arrangements*. Financial Accounting Standards Board.

———. 1987. Statement of Financial Accounting Standards No. 95, *Statement of Cash Flows*. Financial Accounting Standards Board.

———. 1992a. Statement of Financial Accounting Standards No. 106, *Employers' Accounting for Postretirement Benefits Other Than Pensions*. Financial Accounting Standards Board.

———. 1992b. Statement of Financial Accounting Standards No. 109, *Accounting for Income Taxes*. Financial Accounting Standards Board.

———. 1995a. Statement of Financial Accounting Standards No. 121, *Accounting for the Impairment of Long-Lived Assets and for Long-Lived Assets to Be Disposed Of*. Financial Accounting Standards Board.

———. 1995b. Statement of Financial Accounting Standards No. 123, *Accounting for Stock-Based Compensation*. Financial Accounting Standards Board.

———. 2002. Statement of Financial Accounting Standards No. 146, *Accounting for Costs Associated with Exit or Disposal Activities*. Financial Accounting Standards Board.

Feng, Mei. 2003. "Why Do Managers Meet or Slightly Beat Earnings Forecasts? A Rational Explanation." Working paper, University of Michigan.

Finger, Catherine A. 1994. "The Ability of Earnings to Predict Future Earnings and Cash Flows." *Journal of Accounting Research*, vol. 32, no. 2 (Autumn):210–223.

Foster, George. 1977. "Quarterly Accounting Data: Time-Series Properties and Predictive-Ability Results." *Accounting Review*, vol. 52, no. 1 (January):1–21.

Francis, Jennifer, and Katherine Schipper. 1999. "Have Financial Statements Lost Their Relevance?" *Journal of Accounting Research*, vol. 37, no. 2 (Autumn):319–352.

Francis, Jennifer, J. Douglas Hanna, and Linda Vincent. 1996. "Causes and Effects of Discretionary Asset Write-Offs." *Journal of Accounting Research*, vol. 34 (Supplement):117–134.

Francis, Jere R., Edward L. Maydew, and H. Charles Sparks. 1999. "The Role of Big 6 Auditors in the Credible Reporting of Accruals." *Auditing*, vol. 18, no. 2 (Fall):17–34.

Frankel, Richard, Marilyn Johnson, and Karen Nelson. 2002. "The Relation between Auditors' Fees for Non-Audit Services and Earnings Quality." *Accounting Review*, vol. 77 (Supplement):71–105.

Frankel, Richard, Marilyn Johnson, and Douglas J. Skinner. 1999. "An Empirical Examination of Conference Calls as a Voluntary Disclosure Medium." *Journal of Accounting Research*, vol. 37, no. 1 (Spring):133–150.

Frankel, Richard, Maureen McNichols, and G. Peter Wilson. 1995. "Discretionary Disclosure and External Financing." *Accounting Review*, vol. 70, no. 1 (January):135–150.

Freeman, Robert N., and Senyo Y. Tse. 1992. "A Nonlinear Model of Security Price Responses to Unexpected Earnings." *Journal of Accounting Research*, vol. 30, no. 2 (Autumn):185–209.

Gao, Pengjie, and Ronald Shrieves. 2002. "Earnings Management and Executive Compensation: A Case of Overdose of Option and Underdose of Salary?" Working paper, University of Tennessee, Knoxville.

Gaver, Jennifer J., and Jeffrey S. Paterson. 2001. "The Association between External Monitoring and Earnings Management in the Property-Casualty Insurance Industry." *Journal of Accounting Research*, vol. 39, no. 2 (September):269–282.

Gaver, Jennifer J., Kenneth M. Gaver, and Jeffrey R. Austin. 1995. "Additional Evidence on Bonus Plans and Income Management." *Journal of Accounting and Economics*, vol. 19, no. 1 (February):3–28.

Givoly, Dan, and Carla Hayn. 2000. "The Changing Time-Series Properties of Earnings, Cash Flows and Accruals: Has Financial Reporting Become More Conservative?" *Journal of Accounting and Economics*, vol. 29, no. 2 (April):287–320.

Griffin, Paul A. 1977. "The Time-Series Behavior of Quarterly Earnings—Preliminary Evidence." *Journal of Accounting Research*, vol. 15, no. 1 (Spring):71–83.

Hall, Steven C., and William W. Stammerjohan. 1997. "Damage Awards and Earnings Management in the Oil Industry." *Accounting Review*, vol. 72, no. 1 (January):47–65.

Hand, John R.M. 1989. "Did Firms Undertake Debt-Equity Swaps for an Accounting Paper Profit or True Financial Gain?" *Accounting Review*, vol. 64, no. 4 (October):587–623.

Hanlon, Michelle. 2003. "The Persistence and Pricing of Earnings, Accruals and Cash Flows When Firms Have Large Book–Tax Differences." Working paper, University of Michigan.

Hayn, Carla. 1995. "The Information Content of Losses." *Journal of Accounting and Economics*, vol. 20, no. 2 (September):125–153.

Healy, Paul M. 1985. "The Effect of Bonus Schemes on Accounting Decisions." *Journal of Accounting and Economics*, vol. 7, nos. 1–3 (April):85–107.

Healy, Paul M., and Krishna Palepu. 2001. "Information Asymmetry, Corporate Disclosure and the Capital Markets: A Review of the Empirical Disclosure Literature." *Journal of Accounting and Economics*, vol. 31, nos. 1–3 (September):405–440.

Healy, Paul M., and James M. Wahlen. 1999. "A Review of the Earnings Management Literature and Its Implications for Standard Setting." *Accounting Horizons*, vol. 13, no. 4 (December):365–383.

Heflin, Frank, K.R. Subramanyam, and Yuan Zhang. 2003. "Regulation FD and the Financial Information Environment: Early Evidence." *Accounting Review*, vol. 78, no. 1 (January):1–37.

Hirst, D. Eric. 1994. "Auditor Sensitivity to Earnings Management." *Contemporary Accounting Research*, vol. 11, no. 1-II (Fall):405–423.

Hirst, D. Eric, and Patrick E. Hopkins. 1998. "Comprehensive Income Reporting and Analysts' Valuation Judgments." *Journal of Accounting Research*, vol. 36 (Supplement):47–75.

©2004, The Research Foundation of CFA Institute

Holthausen, Robert W., David F. Larcker, and Richard G. Sloan. 1995. "Annual Bonus Schemes and the Manipulation of Earnings." *Journal of Accounting and Economics*, vol. 19, no. 1 (February):29–74.

Hoskin, Robert E., John S. Hughes, and William E. Ricks. 1986. "Evidence on the Incremental Information Content of Additional Firm Disclosures Made Concurrently with Earnings." *Journal of Accounting Research*, vol. 24 (Supplement):1–36.

Hribar, S. Paul. 2001. "The Market Pricing of Components of Accruals." Working paper, Cornell University.

Hribar, Paul, and Daniel W. Collins. 2002. "Errors in Estimating Accruals: Implications for Empirical Research." *Journal of Accounting Research*, vol. 40, no. 1 (March):105–134.

Hung, Mingyi. 2000. "Accounting Standards and Value Relevance of Financial Statements: An International Analysis." *Journal of Accounting and Economics*, vol. 30, no. 3 (December):401–420.

Hutton, Amy P. 2003. "The Determinants and Consequences of Managerial Earnings Guidance Prior to Regulation Fair Disclosure." Working paper, Dartmouth College.

Hutton, Amy P., Gregory S. Miller, and Douglas J. Skinner. 2003. "The Role of Supplementary Statements with Management Earnings Forecasts." *Journal of Accounting Research*, vol. 41, no. 5 (December):867–890.

Imhoff, Eugene A., Jr. 1992. "The Relation between Perceived Accounting Quality and Economic Characteristics of the Firm." *Journal of Accounting and Public Policy*, vol. 11, no. 2 (Summer):97–118.

Imhoff, Eugene A., Jr., and Jacob K. Thomas. 1988. "Economic Consequences of Accounting Standards: The Lease Disclosure Rule Change." *Journal of Accounting and Economics*, vol. 10, no. 4 (December):277–311.

Jaggi, Bikki, and Picheng Lee. 2002. "Earnings Management Response to Debt Covenant Violations and Debt Restructuring." *Journal of Accounting, Auditing and Finance*, vol. 17, no. 4 (Fall):295–324.

Janes, Troy D. 2003. "Accruals, Financial Distress, and Debt Covenants." Working paper, State University of New York at Buffalo.

Jones, Jennifer F. 1991. "Earnings Management during Import Relief Investigations." *Journal of Accounting Research*, vol. 29, no. 2 (Autumn):193–228.

Joy, O. Maurice, Robert H. Litzenberger, and Richard W. McEnally. 1977. "The Adjustment of Stock Prices to Announcements of Unanticipated Changes in Quarterly Earnings." *Journal of Accounting Research*, vol. 15, no. 2 (Autumn):207–225.

Kasznik, Ron. 1999. "On the Association between Voluntary Disclosure and Earnings Management." *Journal of Accounting Research*, vol. 37, no. 1 (Spring):57–82.

Kasznik, Ron, and Baruch Lev. 1995. "To Warn or Not to Warn: Management Disclosures in the Face of an Earnings Surprise." *Accounting Review*, vol. 70, no. 1 (January):113–134.

Kasznik, Ron, and Maureen F. McNichols. 2002. "Does Meeting Expectations Matter? Evidence from Analyst Forecast Revisions and Share Prices." *Journal of Accounting Research*, vol. 40, no. 3 (June):727–759.

Kay, Robert S. 1976. "Disagreements under Accounting Series Release No. 165." *Journal of Accountancy*, vol. 142, no. 4 (October):75–82.

Key, Kimberly Galligan. 1997. "Political Cost Incentives for Earnings Management in the Cable Television Industry." *Journal of Accounting and Economics*, vol. 23, no. 3 (November):309–338.

Kim, Oliver, and Robert E. Verrecchia. 1994. "Market Liquidity and Volume around Earnings Announcements." *Journal of Accounting and Economics*, vol. 17, nos. 1/2 (January):41–67.

Kinney, William R., Jr., and Roger D. Martin. 1994. "Does Auditing Reduce Bias in Financial Reporting? A Review of Audit-Related Adjustment Studies." *Auditing*, vol. 13, no. 1 (Spring):149–157.

Kinney, William R., Jr., Zoe-Vonna Palmrose, and Susan Scholz. 2003. "Auditor Independence and Non-Audit Services: What Do Restatements Suggest?" Working paper, University of Texas at Austin.

Klein, April. 2002. "Audit Committee, Board of Director Characteristics, and Earnings Management." *Journal of Accounting and Economics*, vol. 33, no. 3 (August):375–400.

Kormendi, Roger, and Robert Lipe. 1987. "Earnings Innovations, Earnings Persistence, and Stock Returns." *Journal of Business*, vol. 60, no. 3 (July):323–345.

Krishnan, Gopal V. 2003. "Does Big 6 Auditor Industry Expertise Constrain Earnings Management?" *Accounting Horizons*, vol. 17 (Supplement):1–16.

Lakonishok, Josef, Andrei Schleifer, and Robert W. Vishny. 1994. "Contrarian Investment, Extrapolation, and Risk." *Journal of Finance*, vol. 49, no. 5 (December):1541–78.

Lee, Charles M.C., Belinda Mucklow, and Mark J. Ready. 1993. "Spreads, Depths, and the Impact of Earnings Information: An Intraday Analysis." *Review of Financial Studies*, vol. 6, no. 2 (Summer):345–374.

Lee, Chun I., Leonard Rosenthal, and Kimberly Gleason. 2004. "Effect of Regulation FD on Asymmetric Information." *Financial Analysts Journal*, vol. 60, no. 3 (May/June):79–89.

Leuz, Christian, Dhananjay Nanda, and Peter D. Wysocki. 2003. "Earnings Management and Investor Protection: An International Comparison." *Journal of Financial Economics*, vol. 69, no. 3 (September):505–527.

Lev, Baruch. 1983. "Some Economic Determinants of Time-Series Properties of Earnings." *Journal of Accounting and Economics*, vol. 5, no. 1 (April):31–48.

Lev, Baruch, and Doron Nissim. 2002. "Institutional Investors and the Accrual Anomaly." Working paper, Columbia University.

Lev, Baruch and Ramu S. Thiagarajan. 1993. "Fundamental Information Analysis." *Journal of Accounting Research*, vol. 31, no. 2 (Autumn):190–215.

Lev, Baruch, and Paul Zarowin. 1999. "The Boundaries of Financial Reporting and How to Extend Them." *Journal of Accounting Research*, vol. 37, no. 2 (Autumn):353–385.

Liberty, Susan E., and Gerald L. Zimmerman. 1986. "Labor Union Contract Negotiations and Accounting Choices." *Accounting Review*, vol. 61, no. 4 (October):692–712.

Lipe, Robert C. 1986. "The Information Contained in the Components of Earnings." *Journal of Accounting Research*, vol. 24 (Supplement):37–68.

Lipe, Robert C., Lisa Bryant, and Sally K. Widener. 1998. "Do Nonlinearity, Firm-Specific Coefficients, and Losses Represent Distinct Factors in the Relation between Stock Returns and Accounting Earnings?" *Journal of Accounting and Economics*, vol. 25, no. 2 (May):195–214.

Lougee, Barbara A., and Carol A. Marquardt. 2002. "Earnings Quality and Strategic Disclosure: An Empirical Examination of 'Pro Forma' Earnings." Working paper, University of California, Irvine.

Lundholm, Russell, and Richard Sloan. 2003. *MP Equity Valuation and Analysis with eVal CD-ROM*. New York: McGraw-Hill/Irwin.

Lundholm, Russell J., and Terrence B. O'Keefe. 2001. "On Comparing Residual Income and Discounted Cash Flow Models of Equity Valuation: A Response to Penman 2001." *Contemporary Accounting Research*, vol. 18, no. 4 (Winter):693–696.

Makar, Stephen D., Pervaiz Alam, and Michael A. Pearson. 1998. "Antitrust Merger Investigations and the Quality of Reported Earnings." *Journal of Applied Business Research*, vol. 14, no. 4 (Fall):89–100.

Matsumoto, Dawn A. 2002. "Management's Incentives to Avoid Negative Earnings Surprises." *Accounting Review*, vol. 77, no. 3 (July):483–514.

Maydew, Edward L. 1997. "Tax-Induced Earnings Management by Firms with Net Operating Losses." *Journal of Accounting Research*, vol. 35, no. 1 (Spring):83–96.

McConomy, Bruce J. 1998. "Bias and Accuracy of Management Earnings Forecasts: An Evaluation of the Impact of Auditing." *Contemporary Accounting Research*, vol. 15, no. 2 (Summer):167–196.

McDaniel, Linda S., Roger D. Martin, and Laureen A. Maines. 2002. "Evaluating Financial Reporting Quality: The Effects of Financial Expertise versus Financial Literacy." *Accounting Review*, vol. 77 (Supplement):139–167.

McMullen, Dorothy A. 1996. "Audit Committee Performance: An Investigation of the Consequences Associated with Audit Committees." *Auditing*, vol. 15, no. 1 (Spring):87–103.

McVay, Sarah. 2003. "The Use of Special Items to Inflate Earnings." Working paper, University of Michigan.

Mendenhall, Richard R., and Donald H. Fehrs. 1999. "Option Listing and the Stock-Price Response to Earnings Announcements." *Journal of Accounting and Economics*, vol. 27, no. 1 (February):57–87.

Miller, Gregory S. 2002. "Earnings Performance and Discretionary Disclosure." *Journal of Accounting Research*, vol. 40, no. 1 (March):173–204.

———. 2004. "The Press as a Watchdog for Accounting Fraud." Working paper, Harvard Business School.

Minton, Bernadette A., Catherine M. Schrand, and Beverly R. Walther. 2002. "The Role of Volatility in Forecasting." *Review of Accounting Studies*, vol. 7, nos. 2/3 (June):195–215.

Moehrle, Stephen R. 2002. "Do Firms Use Restructuring Charge Reversals to Meet Earnings Targets?" *Accounting Review*, vol. 77, no. 2 (April):397–413.

Moyer, Susan E. 1990. "Capital Adequacy Ratio Regulations and Accounting Choices in Commercial Banks." *Journal of Accounting and Economics*, vol. 13, no. 2 (July):123–154.

Myers, Linda. 2001. "On the Association between Governance and Control Mechanisms and Income-Decreasing Earnings Management." Working paper, University of Michigan.

Myers, Linda A., James N. Myers, and Thomas C. Omer. 2003. "Exploring the Term of the Auditor–Client Relationship and the Quality of Earnings: A Case for Mandatory Auditor Rotation?" *Accounting Review*, vol. 78, no. 3 (July):779–799.

Narayanamoorthy, Ganapathi. 2003. "Conservatism and Cross-Sectional Variation in the Post-Earnings-Announcement Drift." Working paper, Yale School of Management.

Nelson, Mark, John Elliott, and Robin Tarpley. 2003. "How Are Earnings Managed? Examples from Auditors." *Accounting Horizons*, vol. 17 (Supplement):17–35.

Nissim, Doron, and Stephen H. Penman. 2001. "Ratio Analysis and Equity Valuation: From Research to Practice." *Review of Accounting Studies*, vol. 6, no. 1 (March):109–154.

———. 2003. "Financial Statement Analysis of Leverage and How It Informs about Profitability and Price-to-Book Ratios." *Review of Accounting Studies*, vol. 8, no. 4 (December):531–560.

O'Glove, Thornton L. 1987. *Quality of Earnings*. New York: Free Press.

O'Hanlon, John, S. Poon, and R.A. Yaansah. 1992. "Market Recognition of Differences in Earnings Persistence: UK Evidence." *Journal of Business Finance and Accounting*, vol. 19, no. 4 (June):625–639.

Ohlson, James A. 1995. "Earnings, Book Values, and Dividends in Equity Security Valuation." *Contemporary Accounting Research*, vol. 11, no. 2 (Spring):661–687.

Ohlson, James, and Xiao Jun Zhang. 1998. "Accrual Accounting and Equity Valuation." *Journal of Accounting Research*, vol. 36 (Supplement):85–111.

Palepu, Krishna G., Victor L. Bernard, and Paul M. Healy. 2000. *Business Analysis and Valuation: Using Financial Statements*. 2nd ed. Cincinnati, OH: South-Western Publishing.

Palmrose, Zoe-Vonna. 1988. "An Analysis of Auditor Litigation and Audit Service Quality." *Accounting Review*, vol. 63, no. 1 (January):55–73.

Penman, Stephen H. 1980. "An Empirical Investigation of the Voluntary Disclosure of Corporate Earnings Forecasts." *Journal of Accounting Research*, vol. 18, no. 1 (Spring):132–160.

———. 2001a. *Financial Statement Analysis and Security Valuation*. New York: McGraw-Hill/Irwin.

———. 2001b. "On Comparing Cash Flow and Accrual Accounting Models for Use in Equity Valuation: A Response to Lundholm and O'Keefe." *Contemporary Accounting Research*, vol. 18, no. 4 (Winter):681–692.

———. 2003. "The Quality of Financial Statements: Perspectives from the Recent Stock Market Bubble." *Accounting Horizons*, vol. 17 (Supplement):77–96.

Penman, Stephen H., and Theodore Sougiannis. 1998. "A Comparison of Dividend, Cash Flow, and Earnings Approaches to Equity Valuation." *Contemporary Accounting Research*, vol. 15, no. 3 (Fall):343–383.

Penman, Stephen H., and Xiao-Jun Zhang. 2002. "Accounting Conservatism, the Quality of Earnings, and Stock Returns." *Accounting Review*, vol. 77, no. 2 (April):237–264.

Perry, Susan E., and Thomas H. Williams. 1994. "Earnings Management Preceding Management Buyout Offers." *Journal of Accounting and Economics*, vol. 18, no. 2 (September):157–179.

Pourciau, Susan. 1993. "Earnings Management and Nonroutine Executive Changes." *Journal of Accounting and Economics*, vol. 16, nos. 1–3 (January–July):317–336.

Pownall, Grace, and Gregory Waymire. 1989. "Voluntary Disclosure Credibility and Securities Prices: Evidence from Management Earnings Forecasts: 1969–73." *Journal of Accounting Research*, vol. 27, no. 2 (Autumn):227–245.

Pownall, Grace, Charles E. Wasley, and Gregory Waymire. 1993. "The Stock Price Effects of Alternative Types of Management Earnings Forecasts." *Accounting Review*, vol. 68, no. 4 (October):896–912.

Preinreich, G.A.D. 1938. "Annual Survey of Economic Theory: The Theory of Depreciation." *Econometrica*, vol. 6, no. 3 (July):219–241.

Ramesh, K., and S. Ramu Thiagarajan. 1993. "Estimating the Permanent Component of Accounting Earnings Using the Unobservable Components Model: Implications for Price–Earnings Research." *Journal of Accounting, Auditing and Finance*, vol. 8, no. 4 (Fall):399–425.

Rangan, Srinivasan. 1998. "Earnings Management and the Performance of Seasoned Equity Offerings." *Journal of Financial Economics*, vol. 50, no. 1 (October):101–122.

Rangan, Srinivasan, and Richard G. Sloan. 1998. "Implications of the Integral Approach to Quarterly Reporting for the Post-Earnings-Announcement Drift." *Accounting Review*, vol. 73, no. 3 (July):353–371.

Reichelstein, Stefan. 2000. "Providing Managerial Incentives: Cash Flows versus Accrual Accounting." *Journal of Accounting Research*, vol. 38, no. 2 (Autumn):243–269.

Richardson, Scott A. 2003. "Earnings Quality and Short Sellers." *Accounting Horizons*, vol. 17 (Supplement):49–61.

Richardson, Scott A., and Richard G. Sloan. 2003. "External Financing and Future Stock Returns." Working paper, University of Pennsylvania.

Richardson, Scott A., Richard G. Sloan, Mark T. Soliman, and A. Irem Tuna. 2003. "Information in Accruals about the Quality of Earnings." Working paper, University of Michigan.

———. 2004. "The Implications of Accounting Distortions and Growth for Accruals and Profitability." Working paper, University of Michigan.

Richardson, Scott A., Siew Hong Teoh, and Peter D. Wysocki. 2003. "The Walkdown to Beatable Analyst Forecasts: The Roles of Equity Issuance and Insider Trading Incentives." Working paper, University of Pennsylvania.

Richardson, Scott A., A. Irem Tuna, and Min Wu. 2003. "Predicting Earnings Management: The Case of Earnings Restatements." Working paper, University of Pennsylvania.

Rogerson, William P. 1997. "Intertemporal Cost Allocation and Managerial Investment Incentives: A Theory Explaining the Use of Economic Value Added as a Performance Measure." *Journal of Political Economy*, vol. 105, no. 4 (August):770–795.

Ronn, Ehud I., and Avinash K. Verma. 1986. "Pricing Risk-Adjusted Deposit Insurance: An Option-Based Model." *Journal of Finance*, vol. 41, no. 4 (September):871–895.

Rose, Peter S. 1996. *Commercial Bank Management*. New York: Irwin.

Ruddock, Caitlin, Kate Sherwood, and Stephen Taylor. 2004. "Non-Audit Services and Earnings Management: Is Auditor Independence Impaired?" Working paper, University of New South Wales.

Schipper, Katherine. 1989. "Earnings Management." *Accounting Horizons*, vol. 3, no. 4 (December):91–102.

Schipper, Katherine, and Linda Vincent. 2003. "Earnings Quality." *Accounting Horizons*, vol. 17 (Supplement):97–110.

Scholes, Myron S., G. Peter Wilson, and Mark A. Wolfson. 1990. "Tax Planning, Regulatory Capital Planning, and Financial Reporting Strategy for Commercial Banks." *Review of Financial Studies*, vol. 3, no. 4 (Winter):625–650.

———. 1992. "Firms' Responses to Anticipated Reductions in Tax Rates: The Tax Reform Act of 1986." *Journal of Accounting Research*, vol. 30 (Supplement):161–191.

Schrand, Catherine M., and Beverly R. Walther. 2000. "Strategic Benchmarks in Earnings Announcements: The Selective Disclosure of Prior-Period Earnings Components." *Accounting Review*, vol. 75, no. 2 (April):151–177.

Schrand, Catherine M., and Franco M.H. Wong. 2003. "Earnings Management Using the Valuation Allowance for Deferred Tax Assets under SFAS No. 109." *Contemporary Accounting Research*, vol. 20, no. 3 (Fall):579–611.

Serwer, Andy. 2002. "Kodak: In the Noose." *Fortune* (4 February):147–148.

Shane, Phil, Naomi Soderstrom, and Sung Wook Yoon. 2001. "Reg FD, Analysts' Forecasts and the Information Environment." Working paper, University of Colorado.

Shivakumar, Lakshmanan. 2000. "Do Firms Mislead Investors by Overstating Earnings before Seasoned Equity Offerings?" *Journal of Accounting and Economics*, vol. 29, no. 3 (June):339–371.

Skinner, Douglas J. 1990. "Options Markets and the Information Content of Accounting Earnings Releases." *Journal of Accounting and Economics*, vol. 13, no. 3 (October):191–211.

———. 1994. "Why Firms Voluntarily Disclose Bad News." *Journal of Accounting Research*, vol. 32, no. 1 (Spring):38–60.

———. 2003. "Should Firms Disclose Everything to Everybody? A Discussion of 'Open vs. Closed Conference Calls: The Determinants and Effects of Broadening Access to Disclosure'." *Journal of Accounting and Economics*, vol. 34, nos. 1–3 (January):181–187.

Skinner, Douglas J., and Richard G. Sloan. 2002. "Earnings Surprises, Growth Expectations, and Stock Returns or Don't Let an Earnings Torpedo Sink Your Portfolio." *Review of Accounting Studies*, vol. 7, nos. 2/3 (June):289–312.

Sloan, Richard G. 1996. "Do Stock Prices Fully Reflect Information in Accruals and Cash Flows about Future Earnings?" *Accounting Review*, vol. 71, no. 3 (July):289–315.

Soffer, Leonard C., S. Ramu Thiagarajan, and Beverly R. Walther. 2000. "Earnings Preannouncement Strategies." *Review of Accounting Studies*, vol. 5, no. 1 (March):5–26.

Soliman, Mark. 2003. "Using Industry-Adjusted DuPont Analysis to Predict Future Profitability." Working paper, Stanford University.

Storey, Reed K., and Sylvia Storey. 1998. *The Framework of Financial Accounting Concepts and Standards*. Special report to the Financial Accounting Standards Board (January).

Subramanyam, K.R. 1996a. "The Pricing of Discretionary Accruals." *Journal of Accounting and Economics*, vol. 22, nos. 1–3 (August):249–281.

———. 1996b. "Uncertain Precision and Price Reactions to Information." *Accounting Review*, vol. 71, no. 2 (April):207–220.

Subramanyam, K.R., and Mohan Venkatachalam. 1998. "The Role of Book Value in Equity Valuation: Does the Stock Variable Merely Proxy for Relevant Past Flows?" Working paper, University of Southern California.

Subramanyam, K.R., and John J. Wild. 1996. "Going-Concern Status, Earnings Persistence, and Informativeness of Earnings." *Contemporary Accounting Research*, vol. 13, no. 1 (Spring):251–273.

Sweeney, Amy P. 1994. "Debt-Covenant Violations and Managers' Accounting Responses." *Journal of Accounting and Economics*, vol. 17, no. 3 (May):281–308.

Tan, Hun-Tong, Robert Libby, and James E. Hunton. 2002. "Analysts' Reactions to Earnings Preannouncement Strategies." *Journal of Accounting Research*, vol. 40, no. 1 (March):223–246.

Tasker, Sarah C. 1998. "Bridging the Information Gap: Quarterly Conference Calls as a Medium for Voluntary Disclosure." *Review of Accounting Studies*, vol. 3, nos. 1/2:137–167.

Teoh, Siew Hong, and T.J. Wong. 1993. "Perceived Auditor Quality and the Earnings Response Coefficient." *Accounting Review*, vol. 68, no. 2 (April):346–367.

———. 2002. "Why New Issuers and High-Accrual Firms Underperform: The Role of Analysts' Credulity." *Review of Financial Studies*, vol. 15, no. 3 (Summer):869–900.

Teoh, Siew Hong, Ivo Welch, and T.J. Wong. 1998a. "Earnings Management and the Long-Run Market Performance of Initial Public Offerings." *Journal of Finance*, vol. 53, no. 6 (December):1935–74.

————. 1998b. "Earnings Management and the Underperformance of Seasoned Equity Offerings." *Journal of Financial Economics*, vol. 50, no. 1 (October):63–99.

Teoh, Siew Hong, T.J. Wong, and Gita Rao. 1998. "Are Accruals during Initial Public Offerings Opportunistic?" *Review of Accounting Studies*, vol. 3, nos. 1/2:175–208.

Thomas, Jacob K., and Huai Zhang. 2002. "Inventory Changes and Future Returns." *Review of Accounting Studies*, vol. 7, nos. 2/3 (June):163–187.

Verrecchia, Robert E. 2001. "Essays on Disclosure." *Journal of Accounting and Economics*, vol. 32, nos. 1–3 (December):97–180.

Watts, Ross L., and Richard W. Leftwich. 1977. "The Time Series of Annual Accounting Earnings." *Journal of Accounting Research*, vol. 15, no. 2 (Autumn):253–271.

Waymire, Gregory. 1986. "Additional Evidence on the Accuracy of Analyst Forecasts before and after Voluntary Management Earnings Forecasts." *Accounting Review*, vol. 61, no. 1 (January):129–142.

Wild, John J. 1992. "Stock Price Informativeness of Accounting Numbers: Evidence on Earnings, Book Values, and Their Components." *Journal of Accounting and Public Policy*, vol. 11, no. 2 (Summer):119–154.

Williams, Patricia A. 1996. "The Relation between a Prior Earnings Forecast by Management and Analyst Response to a Current Management Forecast." *Accounting Review*, vol. 71, no. 1 (January):103–116.

Wu, Y. Woody. 1997. "Management Buyouts and Earnings Management." *Journal of Accounting, Auditing and Finance*, vol. 12, no. 4 (Fall):373–389.

Xie, Hong. 2001. "The Mispricing of Abnormal Accruals." *Accounting Review*, vol. 76, no. 3 (July):357–373.